Illustrator:
Bruce Hedges

Editor:
Mary Kaye Taggart

Editorial Project Manager:
Karen J. Goldfluss, M.S. Ed.

Editor in Chief:
Sharon Coan, M.S. Ed.

Art Director:
Elayne Roberts

Associate Designer:
Denise Bauer

Cover Artist:
Chris Macabitas

Product Manager:
Phil Garcia

Imaging:
James Edward Grace

Publishers:
Rachelle Cracchiolo, M.S. Ed.
Mary Dupuy Smith, M.S. Ed.

How to Prepare Your Students for
Standardized Tests

Primary

Author:

Julia Jasmine, M.A.

Teacher Created Materials, Inc.
6421 Industry Way
Westminster, CA 92683
www.teachercreated.com
ISBN 1-57690-130-0
©1997 Teacher Created Materials, Inc.
Revised, 1999
Made in U.S.A.

Table of Contents

Table of Contents *(cont.)*

Table of Contents *(cont.)*

Introduction

Traditional standardized tests are back! Returning with them is all of the test anxiety that we thought we had put behind us with the advent of alternative assessment. However, the truth of the matter is that in most cases traditional testing never went away at all. Alternative assessment requirements were simply added to the old methods of assessment. Many school districts continued to use their traditional standardized testing as well as their newer proficiency testing which they added during the last great assessment upheaval. Teachers and their students felt that they were being "tested to death."

So, if standardized testing never really went away, just what is it that is happening now? It would probably be correct to say that what has returned is the emphasis on standardized testing. National standards are important now, and the states that give the right tests at the right times will receive the most money for education from the federal government.

The most realistic way to look at all of this is that there is not much the individual teacher can do about it either way. It will help our students, however, if we keep in mind that the old objections to standardized testing—the ones that made us seek out alternatives in the first place—are still valid:

- This is a big country with a diverse population, and when tests are "normed," the sample population may not reflect this enormous diversity.

- Students who are not naturally talented in the areas of language and math (who do not excel in what Howard Gardner calls the linguistic and logical/mathematical intelligences in *Frames of Mind: The Theory of Multiple Intelligences* [Basic Books, 1983]) will not do well on achievement tests, even if these students may be immensely talented in other areas.

- Students who do not speak and read English fluently will not do well on the tests.

- Students who live in poverty will not have the experiential background to understand the questions on the test.

There are many people in education who can help to solve these problems:

- The test makers can help by keeping their assessment tools free from bias and basing their norms on a sample that is as representative of our population as possible.

- Educational administrators can help by interpreting the test results correctly, keeping in mind the student populations that are being tested, and by explaining their interpretations to the public.

- Teachers can help by giving their students the information they need to pass the tests. Some of this information consists of knowledge, but a great deal of it consists of the test-taking skills, which are the subject of this book.

Test Success

At Least Three Requirements

The ability to do well when taking traditional standardized tests requires at least three things:

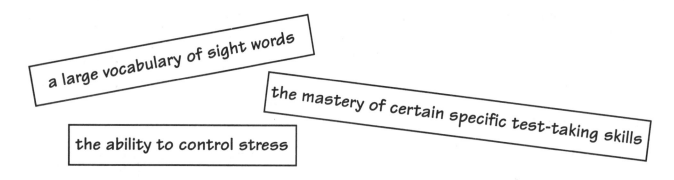

a large vocabulary of sight words

the mastery of certain specific test-taking skills

the ability to control stress

The vocabulary issue is discussed in detail in the section that follows. The test-taking skills, which will be briefly discussed here and reinforced in each relevant practice section, can be taught by teachers, used by students, and have nothing much to do with the stated purpose of the particular test—to determine a student's level in reading or math, for example. Some tools for controlling stress will also be suggested.

Who Needs Test-Taking Skills?

Certainly, all students need test-taking skills, but "good" students may need them most of all. For example, without test-taking ability, fluent readers may score low on the incremental skills that have been identified as necessary building blocks for beginning readers. These fluent readers are well past the place where they labor over, or are even really aware of, beginning and ending sounds. They just read. Similarly, students with excellent skills in logic and problem solving may not show much success on problems involving the basic math facts that are often learned by rote.

These, of course, are the very students you would like to have excel when they take whatever test your school or district has decided to give. They should be able to carry records of success with them in their school careers, and you should get credit for teaching them. This is particularly important in an educational climate where school districts, schools, and even individual teachers are judged on their students' test results which are often emblazoned across the newspapers to generate reactions from people who have no idea what they mean or how to interpret them.

What Are These Skills?

The skills that students need in order to do well on standardized tests include the ability to follow complicated and often confusing directions, the ability to scale back what they know and focus on just what is asked of them, the ability to choose among confusing distracters (multiple-choice answers), and the ability to maintain concentration during boring and tedious repetition. (You have probably spent years perfecting your ability to give clear and easily understood directions, and you probably love it when your students bring their existing knowledge to bear on a new problem. Likewise, you probably give your students clear answer choices from which to choose, and you undoubtedly do not want to change your basic teaching style to one that is boring and repetitious. Obviously, you will need different approaches.)

Test Success *(cont.)*

What to Do and How to Do It

You can teach your students to translate the test directions into the words that you use and that they understand. You can show them how to restrict their responses (no application or synthesis). You can turn the tedium into a game. You can teach test-taking skills during a separate segment of your school day and set up some kind of a reward system to help your students stay focused. The material that follows in this book will help you to do all of these things without having a negative impact on your curriculum or individual teaching style.

Inform the Students

Be sure to explain to the students what you are doing and why. Tell them that you will be teaching test-taking skills to them, establishing a room environment much like what they will experience during a real test, and often reading from a script. Assure them that the experience will reduce their stress levels and make them successful test takers. (Assure yourself that the experience will reduce your stress level too and make you look good when the scores are published in your local newspaper or produced as part of your own yearly evaluation.)

Address the Issue of Stress

Give your students some tools for handling the stress that accompanies test taking. Talk about routine habits that they can develop: getting enough sleep, eating a good breakfast, and getting some exercise after school. Even small children know they feel better after they use their large muscles by running, jumping, climbing, and so on. Consider sending home a letter encouraging parents to become part of the testing team by helping their students develop these habits.

Allow self-directed activities and free movement around your classroom when you are not presenting teacher-directed activities. In this way you will prevent the school day from turning into one long paper-and-pencil session.

Tell the students that they can use their imaginations to see themselves doing well on tests. Many athletes use this technique and have written or talked about it at length. They "see" themselves hitting the ball, making the basket, or winning the race. Read to your students some of these accounts and encourage them to see themselves feeling calm, thinking clearly, and marking the correct answers.

Use exercises such as deep breathing and stretching at regular intervals during the day. Try using a "Simon Says" format with young children. Then, when the test time arrives, your students will be familiar with testing and will not be distracted because of the novelty of the activity.

The Vocabulary Piece

Sight Vocabulary

The size of your students' sight vocabularies will be a deciding factor in how well they score on standardized achievement tests. The term *sight vocabulary* is used here to mean words that students do not have to stop and figure out. There simply will not be time to apply decoding skills, no matter what they happen to be or how well your students can use them, to all of the words in the test. They must know not only the target words in vocabulary questions but also all of the words used in the stories and all of the words used in the distracters (multiple-choice answers). For example, if students cannot correctly read all of the possible answers in a question about rhyming words, they will not be able to answer the question.

Depending on the format of the test you are giving, you may be able to encourage your students to answer all of the questions that contain words that they do know and then go back and use their decoding skills to figure out words that they did not recognize. However, because of time constraints, you may not always be able to offer this option to them.

Some Methods to Use

Whatever decoding skills or combinations of decoding skills you are using, consider adding some of these practice methods to increase your students' sight vocabularies. **Flashcards** are a wonderful, if old-fashioned, tool. So is **labeling** everything (a practice in which you write the names of everything in your classroom on cards or sentence strips and actually stick these labels on the objects). **Oral discussion** of words is a handy method that can be used as a part of instruction in any subject matter. Consider posting a **list** of words to accompany a social studies or science lesson or to provide a recall tool for the words you talked about in an oral discussion. Finally, give your students a **visual context** for as many words as possible.

Flashcards

Gather words for vocabulary flashcards from all of the sources that are available to you. Just write the words on ordinary 3" x 5" or 5" x 7" index cards. You can play "Around the World" with these cards as a teacher-directed activity or put packs of the flashcards in your activity centers for your students to use in partner or small group play. Also, you can have classroom aides, volunteers, or cross-age tutors use the flashcards with individuals or small groups.

Depending on how many words you manage to gather, you can pack them according to categories: Basal Reader, Prepositions, Plurals, and so on. (See "Some Sources for Words" starting on page 11.)

The Vocabulary Piece *(cont.)*

Labeling

Sit down with a stack of cards or strips and look around the room. Write a label for everything you see: wall, door, light switch, window, windowsill, teacher's desk, student's desk, table, floor, bookcase, book, pen, pencil, paper, and on and on. You can do this by yourself, or you can do it with the students, having them read a word before taping it in the right place. Put loops of tape on the back of each card or strip so that the students can simply press them in place.

Use "reading the room" as a sponge activity when you have a minute or two to fill while waiting to go somewhere, such as an assembly or the computer lab.

Ask your principal if you can label the office, the cafeteria, and/or the multipurpose room. Then you can "read the school" as you walk to and from lunch and assemblies.

The added benefit of this method is that each word has a concrete object attached to it.

Oral Discussion

This is the easiest of all the methods, requiring no supplies or setup. Just stop and talk about the words you are hearing or reading. (Consider reinforcing this method by jotting the words down on the chalkboard as you talk about them.) For example, if someone reads, hears, or says the word *stream*, you could initiate discussion with the following questions.

What is a stream?

How does a stream compare to a river?

What is a creek?

Who has ever seen a stream, a river, or a creek?

What did it (they) look like?

What are the differences among streams, rivers, and creeks and bodies of water like oceans or lakes?

Who has seen an ocean or a lake?

What did it (they) look like?

The added benefit of this method is that each word automatically has a basic concept attached to it.

The Vocabulary Piece *(cont.)*

Lists

If you had been making a list of the preceding oral discussion, you would have these words:

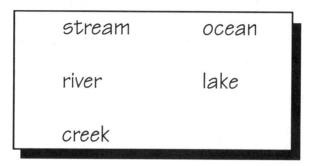

Depending on the original source of the word "stream"—if it is part of a science lesson about bodies of water, for example—and depending on how many other words you stop to discuss, you might come up with quite an extensive list of words.

List all of these words on a chart entitled "Bodies of Water." Post it somewhere in the classroom and review it occasionally.

Visual Context

Provide your students with a visual context for the words that they learn by showing and discussing as many videos and movies as you can fit into your busy day. Show science films, social studies films, math films, and films based on classic or modern stories. In order to make this method work, you will need to look at the movie or video with your class. Make a practice of stopping the projector or VCR to talk about the words. No matter what kind of a film or video you are watching, if your class had participated in the science lesson mentioned above you could stop it and say:

> Look. This is a river. This is what a river looks like in a city (or in a rural setting). I'll rewind the tape so that we can look at it again. Remember, we wrote the word "river" on our chart of "Bodies of Water." (Ask someone to go to the chart and point out the written word.)

Try not to be pressured into feeling guilty for showing videos and movies to your students. Some people feel that anything visual is merely entertainment and object to this in the classroom. If you are faced with this kind of criticism, you can counter it by pointing out that you are using the visual experiences as part of your instructional method to maximize your students' success on the upcoming standardized tests by helping them to increase their vocabularies. If necessary, invite your critics to sit in on a lesson in which you do vocabulary exercises, using additional visual aids.

The Vocabulary Piece *(cont.)*

Some Sources for Words

You can get your words from anywhere and everywhere. For purposes of standardized testing, in addition to what might be called **grade-level words**, your students will need to know **subject-specific words**, words that may be **outside of their personal experiential backgrounds**, **plural forms of words**, **words with affixes**, **compound words**, **contractions**, **synonyms and antonyms**, **words with more than one meaning**, and **prepositions and their meanings**. They will also need a strategy for dealing with a variety of **proper names** and know how the word **"blank"** is used in many standardized test questions.

Grade-Level Words

If you are using a basal reader series, a good source of grade-level words is the word list that usually appears at the back of the book or in the teacher's materials. You should also provide yourself with the word lists from the preceding books in the series. For example, if you are using a third grade reader, get the word lists from the second and first grade readers and the primers and pre-primers as well. If these lists are not provided, call the publisher's customer representative and ask for them.

If you are using other kinds of reading materials—a literature-based program for example—skim through the books and choose the words that you think are the most relevant. Also, get words from other standard lists: contact publishers and ask for the word lists for their basal series; use the Dolch list which you can probably find in a teacher supply store; use the EDL list which contains the words appearing at different grade levels in the most used basal reader series; purchase some of the teacher and/or parent resource books containing basic word lists. Also, if you are fairly new to the field of teaching, talk to teachers on your staff who have been teaching for awhile and who may be willing to share their resources. They probably have words lists tucked away in their files, dating from the last time the educational pendulum swung in the direction of standardized testing.

Subject-Specific Words

Since students understand big words as easily as little ones, use the special vocabularies of the subjects you deal with as you teach. Talk about "numerals" as well as "numbers." Use words like "addend," "sum," "difference," and "product" routinely so that your students will be used to them. Talk about "transportation" and "communication" during social studies. Say that you are going to "observe" or "experiment" when beginning a science activity. Add math words, science words, and social studies words to your flashcards and lists. Most math, science, and social studies texts include glossaries. These are excellent sources for important words.

The Vocabulary Piece *(cont.)*

Words Based on Experiential Background

Students need to comprehend the meanings of many words that will not be part of their experiential backgrounds. For example, rural students will need some conceptual context for words such as "subway" and "skyscraper." Suburban students may need to recognize the meanings of such words as "apartment" and "taxi." Urban students, especially those who live in the inner city, should be given some idea of what split-level tract houses and suburban shopping malls look like along with the more obviously rural stables and pastures.

Students in many parts of the South and Southwest may need to be given some information about snow. They may know that it is white, but they will not necessarily know that it is cold. Students who live away from the coasts may have no concept to go with the word "ocean," and students who live on the Great Plains may need to be given some idea of what mountains look like.

Keep in mind that it is always safer to assume that students *do not* have an experiential background than that they *do*. Just because you live only 30 miles from the ocean or the mountains does not mean that your students have ever been to those places.

Lists of words based on experiential background (or the lack of it) will be lists that you develop for your own situation, based on the needs that you identify. The methods described in developing visual contexts for words (see page 10) will be of use here, as will oral discussion. Choose films that will fill in some of your students' blank places. Once you decide on the words you need, you can apply the other methods for reinforcement by making lists and flashcards.

If you are in a situation that allows for field trips, these will help your students to develop experiential backgrounds and enrich their vocabularies. When you know where you are going, prepare a list of words that reflect the things that you think you will see and give a copy of the list to each student. Make sure that they can read the words on the list by reviewing and discussing them as often as is necessary. (Add some little pictures to help younger students to remember the words.) Take the lists with you. Have your students look for the things on the list and check off the ones they find. They can also add words to their lists. (Remember to take pencils.) When you get back from the field trip, talk about what all of the words mean and add them to your flashcards and/or make a list entitled "Our Field Trip."

Note: On page 220 you will find a list of selected words that may be added to your spelling program throughout the year. Since these words often appear on standardized tests, it would benefit students to become familiar with them prior to taking a test.

The Vocabulary Piece *(cont.)*

Plurals

On standardized tests, students are expected to be able to differentiate between the singular and plural forms of both written words and words given orally and then to use these differences in comprehension questions. A statement on a primary test might read, "The boys are playing ball." The three pictures accompanying this statement may consist of one boy holding a bell, one boy playing ball, and two boys playing ball. The students who catch the differences between "bell" and "ball" are apt to fall into the trap of choosing the first picture they see with a ball in it. Rather, they should continue looking until they get to the third picture which reflects the use of the plural, "boys."

When you talk about words, talk about their plurals too. Add plurals to your flashcards and word lists.

Words with Affixes

Students need to be able to read and know the meanings of words with affixes because they will be asked to recognize the *root* word. For example, if the given word is "careful" and two of the distracters are "care" and "car," the student who cannot read the given word with comprehension will not know which answer to choose.

Students also must know the meanings of the suffixes themselves and understand how they affect the meanings of the root words. Remember that the "s" or "es" that forms a plural on the end of a word is considered a suffix.

Have your students add prefixes and suffixes to words for practice. Talk about comparatives and superlatives and have the students add "er" and "est" to words that they already know (for example: slow, slower, slowest).

Compound Words

Compound words are made up of two parts that can each stand alone. Students must be able to distinguish compound words from words with prefixes and suffixes. Have your students brainstorm a list of compound words and use them to make lists and packs of flashcards. Help them to get started with sports words: baseball, basketball, football, etc.

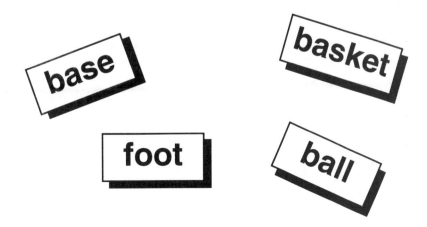

The Vocabulary Piece *(cont.)*

Contractions

The students will be expected to know the words that are represented by common contractions. Do not forget "let's," "I'll," "won't," and "you're." Put a contraction on one side of a flashcard and the words it represents on the other side so that your students can quiz each other.

Synonyms and Antonyms

Both synonyms and antonyms for words can be generated during oral discussions. Make a game of listing them and talk about the fact that synonyms mean the same (or almost the same) as a given word and antonyms mean the opposite.

Words with More Than One Meaning

Words of this type are best demonstrated with an example of a test item.

> Fill in the circle next to the answer that fits best in the blanks in both sentences.
>
> The children _____ into the pool.
>
> The _____ flew into the barn.
>
> ○ bird   ○ dove
> ○ jumped   ○ played

Some of the words fit into one sentence or the other, but only one word fits into both sentences.

Prepositions

In order to be successful when taking standardized tests, students need to know (read and understand the meanings of) all of the common prepositions. One easy way to deal with this need is to approach it in terms of opposites: up/down, in/out, over/under, around/through, before/after, to/from, and so on.

If you make flashcards of these words, add a graphic of some kind to help your students remember the words.

The Vocabulary Piece *(cont.)*

Proper Names

Your students will encounter many proper names in sentences and stories, and not all of these will be of the "Dick and Jane" variety. Many unusual names are used as well as many that reflect a range of ethnic diversity. Meeting an unfamiliar proper name, especially as the very first word of a sentence or story, often has the effect of stopping students in their tracks. You can teach them to substitute the word "blank" (see the next section) for the names they do not know. You can also make them familiar with the written forms of the names of all of the students in your classroom and point out all of the proper names when you read stories.

Not being able to read proper names correctly is a real problem only when the gender of the person named is vital for comprehension. For example, if a statement reads, "Bruce and Billy are smiling," and the pictures show one boy smiling, a boy and a girl smiling, and two boys smiling, it would be imperative that the test taker know that "Bruce" and "Billy" are both boys' names. There is not much you can do about this except expose your students to a number of proper names. (In addition, you should probably make your students aware of the fact that hair length is usually used to show the difference between boys and girls in the test pictures that show only faces.)

"Blank"

The use of the word "blank" is both a test-taking and a vocabulary issue. Many oral questions are asked using the word "blank," and many written questions are set up with a blank (_____) in them. For example, you might be asked to say, "Read the story and the sentence below it. Choose the words that go in the blank."

Maria went to the store for her mother.
She bought some bread.
When she got back home, her mother made a sandwich for her.

Maria bought_____for her mother.

○ the store
○ some bread
○ back home
○ a sandwich

The Vocabulary Piece *(cont.)*

Teach your students to read the statement to themselves, using the word "blank":

Maria bought *blank* for her mother.

Then have them read the statement, putting each answer choice in place of the blank:

Maria bought *the store* for her mother.

Maria bought *some bread* for her mother.

Maria bought *back home* for her mother.

Maria bought *a sandwich* for her mother.

Stress the importance of reading all of the choices in this way and also of checking back in the story before making a decision. The sentence should not only make sense but it should also reflect comprehension of the story.

If your students do not recognize the proper name "Maria," have them read the story to themselves like this:

Blank went to the store for her mother.

Maximizing Vocabulary Results

Send the word lists home with the students:
- Make them part of your homework.
- Use them for spelling words.
- Check out the packs of flashcards to your students in the same way you might check out library books.
- Use the words as the basis for storywriting.

Have contests with prizes (stickers, candy, free time, etc.):

- Who can read a pack of words?
- Who can read the most packs of words?
- Who can tell the meanings of these words?
- Who can add a new word to this list?
- Who can say a rhyming word for each of these words?
- Who can write a rhyming word for each of these words?

The Vocabulary Piece *(cont.)*

Have the students teach each other:

- As soon as one student has mastered a list or a pack of words, have him or her teach those words to another student.
- As soon as one student has mastered a list or a pack of words, have him or her teach those words to a small group of students.

Have students play and/or create games:

- Give your students cards to make double sets of word packs. Have them use the double packs to play "Memory."

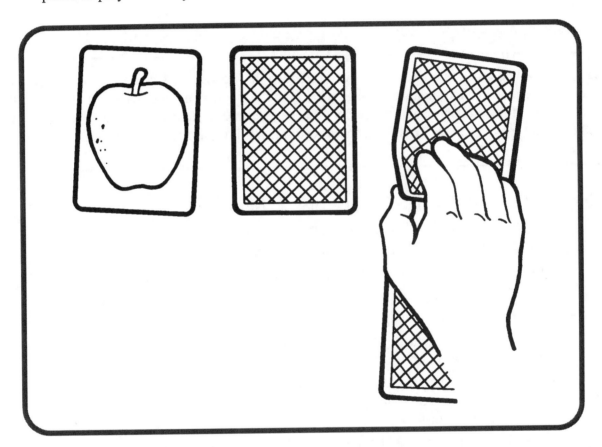

- Play "20 Questions" with words from your lists. (I'm thinking of a word on our list of math words . . . .)
- Give your students the opportunity to make up word games and to teach them to the class.

Keep in mind that gathering words for your word lists is an ongoing process. Try to add to your list every day and use the various methods suggested in this section. Many of the methods can be approached as sponge activities to make your school day more fun. They will also help your students ease into a richer sight vocabulary that will increase their chances for success on standardized tests.

How to Use This Book

Where to Start

1. Consult the appropriate chart for the test you will be giving. (See "Skill Charts" beginning on page 20 for some general information.)

2. Look down the list of skills that appear on that test. You will find page numbers referring you to the Student Practice Pages (SPP) that address each skill. If you will be giving the CTBS "Primary" test, for example, you will find that the first skill listed is **Visual Recognition: Letters**. If you are giving either of the CTBS "Book A" tests (the original or the revised edition), the first skill listed is **Word Analysis/Attack: Beginning Sounds**. If you are using "Book 2—Revised Edition" of the Iowa Test of Basic Skills (ITBS), the first skill listed is **Reading: Vocabulary**.

3. Identify the pages you will be using.

Note: Abbreviated cross-references have been provided throughout the student practice pages and the teacher scripts. To find the teacher page for any Student Practice Page (pages 31–156), see the box at the top of the student page marked TS (Teacher Script). To locate the student page for any Teacher Script (pages 157–217), see the box next to the skill title marked SPP (Student Practice Page).

Making Practice Test Booklets/Scripts/Answer Keys

1. Use the pages you have identified to make a practice test booklet for each of your students.

2. Put your practice test booklets together by following these steps:
   - Make one copy of each of the Student Practice Pages (SPP) you have selected.
   - Assemble the Student Practice Pages in the order that they appear on the chart.
   - Number the pages in the upper right-hand corner.
   - If you want your students to stop at the bottom of a page, add a stop sign. If you want them to go ahead, draw an arrow.
   - When the pages are arranged and numbered and you have added any symbols you need, make enough copies for your students and staple the pages together in booklet form. Do not forget to make one or two extras for yourself.

3. Put your Teacher Script (TS) booklet together by following these steps:
   - Identify and copy the Teacher Script for each Student Practice Page you selected.
   - Several scripts appear on many of the script pages. If you do not need one or more of the scripts on a page you have selected, draw an "X" through the part(s) you will not be using.
   - Assemble the script pages in the same order as the Student Practice Pages.
   - Compare your script pages to the student booklet and write the page numbers from the Student Practice Pages onto the appropriate blanks in your script.
   - Staple the script pages together in booklet form.
   - An answer key is provided on pages 218–224. You can use this key or make your own answer key by marking the correct answers in one of your extra student practice booklets.

How to Use This Book *(cont.)*

Follow-Up

As you use the practice pages, if you come across a skill that is hard for your students, try these ideas:

- Teach the skill in various ways in your regular curriculum.
- Create additional supplementary practice pages of your own.
- Discuss the skill and then retest at a later date, using the practice page in this book.

Teaching the Test-Taking Skills

1. Set aside a block of time each day to teach test skills, using the booklets you have made.

2. Provide time for the students to use the restrooms *before* you start. Anxious students need to use the restrooms more often.

3. Make your room environment as test-like as possible.
   - If your desks are pushed together in groups, have the students move them apart.
   - Put a "Testing—Do Not Disturb" sign on the door.
   - Explain "test etiquette" to your students:
     –no talking
     –attentive listening
     –following directions (such as, "Stop working and put your pencil down.")

4. Show your students how to darken in the circles below their answer choices. Practice on the board and on paper. Tell them that some tests will have ovals rather than circles.

5. Provide a strip of construction paper for each student to use as a page marker. These can double as bookmarks when your testing practice is finished for the day. Make extras for replacements.

6. Provide scratch paper and encourage the students to use it. This is really necessary for math questions and comes in handy for some language arts items too.

7. Establish a routine for replacing broken pencils. Give each student two pencils to start with and have a back-up pencil supply handy. Tell the students that they will need to raise their broken pencils in their hands so that you can give them new ones and take the broken ones without any disturbance. Ask a student or two to take on the job of keeping the pencils sharpened. If your school is short of funds for classroom supplies, send home a letter to ask parents to provide pencils. Pencils break. Students who are worried about your reaction to their broken pencils will not do as well on the test. You cannot relieve all test anxiety, but you *can* relieve "pencil anxiety."

8. Explain to your students that you will be reading from a script and repeating directions and questions in a way that may not sound like your usual teaching style.

9. Explain typical test symbols, such as the arrow that means continue and the stop sign, usually at the bottom of a page, that means do not continue.

10. If applicable to the test pages you are using, explain the answer choice that indicates that the correct answer does not appear. This choice is sometimes found on the math pages.

Skill Charts

Find the Right Test

Look at the charts on pages 21 through 30. The headings on the charts indicate the type of test (CTBS, ITBS, MAT, etc.) that you will be giving as well as the edition (Revised Edition, Fourth Edition, etc.).

In General

In general, the older editions of the tests include two booklets at the primary level, one called "Primary" (usually for grades K–1) and an overlapping test booklet called "Book A" which is for either grades 1–2 or 1–3. The later editions of the tests are usually numbered ("Book 1," "Book 2," and so on). In these books, Book 1 is K–1 and Book 2 applies to either grades 1–2, or just grade 2.

In the older editions, there is a tremendous jump in skill level between "Primary" (K–1) and "Book A" which may be for grades 1–3 or even grades 1–4. If you are testing first graders in a "Book A" (1–3 or 1–4) test, you will need to prepare them for the fact that there will be a lot of material that they will probably not know.

Test Editions and Levels

CAT	***Third Edition [Level]*** Primary (K–1) [10, 11] Book A (1–4) [11, 12, 13]	***Fourth Edition [Level]*** Book 1 (K–1) [10, 11] Book 2 (2) [12]
CTBS	***Old Edition*** Primary (K–1) Book A (1–3)	***Revised Edition*** Book A (1–3)
ITBS	***Old Edition [Level]*** Primary (K–1) [5, 6] Book A (1–2/3) [7, 8/9]	***Revised Edition [Level]*** Book 1 (K–1) [5, 6] Book 2 (2) [7, 8]
MAT	***Third Edition*** Book A (1–3)	***Fourth Edition*** Book 1 (P1) Book 2 (P2)
SAT	Primary (K–1) Book A (1–3)	
TAAS	Grade 3	

A Look at Skills Tested in CAT: Third Edition

Primary (K–1)		Book A (1–4)	
Skill	**Page**	**Skill**	**Page**
Visual/Auditory Recognition		**Word Analysis/Attack**	
Letters	31–33	Beginning Sounds	36, 39
Letter Groups/Words/Word Pairs	34, 35	Ending Sounds	37, 40
Word Analysis/Attack		Vowel Sounds	42
Beginning Sounds	36	Sight Words/Vocabulary	44
Ending Sounds	37	Root Words/Affixes	47–49, 61
Rhyming Sounds	38	Compound Words	45
Beginning Consonants	39	**Vocabulary/Words**	
Ending Consonants	40	Categories/Meanings	55–57
Vowel Sounds	42	Similar Meanings	58
Silent Letters	43	Opposite Meanings	59
Sight Words/Vocabulary	44	In Context	64
Vocabulary/Words		Multiple Meanings	62, 63
Categories	55–57	**Comprehension**	
Meanings	53, 54	Sentences	70–72
In Context	54, 64	Stories	73–85
With Similar Meanings	58	**Spelling**	
Comprehension		Spelling Skills	87
Listening	65, 66	**Language**	
Sentences	70–72	Mechanics	
Stories	73–85	Capitalization	93
Language		Punctuation	97
Usage	50	Capitalization and Punctuation	101, 102
Subject/Predicate	106	Expression	
Statement/Question	107	Usage	50
Math Computation		Sentences	106, 107
Addition	123, 124	Sentence Sequence	111
Subtraction	125, 126	**Math Computation**	
Math Concepts/Applications		Addition	123, 124
Numeration	132	Subtraction	125, 126
Measurement	144–147	Multiplication	127, 128
Geometry	142, 143	Division	129, 130
		Math Concepts/Applications	
		Numeration	132
		Number Families	133
		Number Theory	133–137
		Problem Solving	148–153
		Measurement	144–147
		Geometry	142, 143

A Look at Skills Tested in CAT: Fourth Edition

Book 1 (K–1)		Book 2 (2)	
Skill	**Page**	**Skill**	**Page**
Word Analysis		**Word Analysis**	
Beginning Sounds	36	Word Sounds	36, 37, 39, 40
Ending Sounds	37	Contractions	46
Vowel Sounds	42	Compound Words	45
Sight Words /Vocabulary	44	Root Words/Suffixes	47, 49
Vocabulary		**Vocabulary/Words**	
Pictures	53, 54	Same and Opposite	58, 59
Word Meanings	56	In Context	64, 73–85
Words in Context	64	Multiple Meanings	62, 63
Comprehension		**Comprehension**	
Listening	65, 66	Critical Reading	73, 76, 79, 82, 85
Pictures	67	Stories	73–85
Stories	73–85	**Spelling**	
Language Mechanics		Spelling Skills	87
Capitalization and Punctuation	101, 102	**Language Mechanics**	
Language Expression		Capitalization	93
Usage	50, 103	Punctuation	97
Sentences	106, 107	Capitalization and Punctuation	101, 102
Paragraphs	112	**Language Expression**	
Math Computation		Usage	50, 103
Addition	123, 124	Sentences	103, 106, 107
Subtraction	125, 126	Paragraphs	112
Math Concepts/Applications		**Math Computation**	
Numeration	132	Addition	123, 124
Geometry	142, 143	Subtraction	125, 126
Measurement	144–147	Multiplication	127, 128
Problem Solving	148–153	**Math Concepts/Applications**	
		Numeration	132
		Geometry	142, 143
		Measurement	144–147
		Problem Solving	148–153

A Look at Skills Tested in CTBS: (K–3)

Skill	Primary (K–1) Page	Book A (1–3) Page	Revised Edition Book A (1–3) Page
Visual Recognition			
Letters	31–33		
Letter Groups and Words	34		
Word Analysis/Attack			
Beginning Sounds	36	36	36
Beginning Consonants	39		
Rhyming Sounds	38		
Ending Sounds		37	37
Ending Consonants	40		
Vowel Sounds		42	42
Sight Words/Vocabulary	44	44	44
Syllables		51	
Roots and Affixes		47–52, 61	47–52, 61
Compounds/Contractions		45, 46	45, 46
Vocabulary			
Word Categories	55–57	55–57	55–57
Word Meanings	53–64	53–64	53–64
Similar Meanings		58	58
Opposite Meanings			59
Suffix Meanings			60, 61
More Than One		62, 63	62, 63
Pictures in Context	54		
Words in Context	64	64	64
Reading Comprehension			
Listening	65, 66		65, 66
Sentences	70–72	70–72	70–72
Reality and Fantasy			73–85
Pictures	67		
Stories	73–85	73–85	73–85
Spelling			
Skills		87	87
Language Mechanics			
Capitalization		93	
Punctuation		97	
Capitalization and Punctuation			101, 102
Language Expression			
Usage		50, 103	50, 103
Pronouns			105
Sentences		106, 107	106, 107
Paragraphs			112

A Look at Math Skills Tested in CTBS: (K–3)

Skill	Primary (K–1) Page	Book A (1–3) Page	Revised Edition Book A (1–3) Page
Computation			
Addition		123, 124	123, 124
Subtraction		125, 126	125, 126
Multiplication		127, 128	
Division		129, 130	
Concepts/Applications			
Numeration	132	132	132
Number Sentences/Theory		133–137	
Geometry	142, 143	142, 143	142, 143
Measurement	144–147	144–147	144–147
Problem Solving	148–153	148–153	148–153

A Look at Skills Tested in ITBS: (K–1)

| Primary (K–1) | | Revised Edition Book 1 (K–1) | |

Skill	Page	Skill	Page
Visual and Auditory Recognition		**Vocabulary**	
Letters	31–33	Vocabulary Skills	54, 55
Beginning Sounds	36	**Word Analysis**	
Ending Sounds	37	Letter Recognition	31–33
Rhyming Sounds	38	Initial Sounds	36
Word Analysis		Rhyming Words	38
Beginning Consonants	39	Word Formation	41
Consonant Substitutions	41	**Language Arts**	
Vocabulary		Listening Skills	65, 66
Word Categories	55–57	Language Skills	55–57
Words for Pictures	54	**Math**	
Word Meanings	54	Math Skills	
Comprehension		Patterns/Sequence/Order	131
Listening	65, 66	Numeration	132
Word Recognition	68	Geometry	142, 143
Picture Words	53	Measurement	144–147
Sentences	70–72	Word Problems	148–153
Word Attack	69	**Reading**	
Picture Stories	67	Words	68
Language		Pictures	53, 67
Understanding Language	55–57	Word Attack	69
Usage	53, 54	Sentences	70–72
Math Computation		Reading Comprehension	73–85
Addition	123, 124		
Subtraction	125, 126		
Math Concepts/Applications			
Numeration	132		
Measurement	144–147		
Geometry	142, 143		
Problem Solving	148–153		

A Look at Skills Tested in ITBS: (1–2/3)

Book A (1–2/3)		Revised Edition Book 2 (2)	
Skill	**Page**	**Skill**	**Page**
Vocabulary		**Reading**	
Words for Pictures	53	Vocabulary	53, 54
Word Meanings	56, 62	Word Analysis/Attack	36–43
Word Analysis		Words in Context	64
Consonant Sounds	36, 39	Picture Comprehension	67
Vowel Sounds	42	Reading Comprehension	73–85
Rhyming Sounds	38	**Language Arts**	
Silent Letters	43	Listening Skills	65, 66
Substitutions	41	Language Skills	55–57
Endings	52	Spelling	92
Compounds	45	Capitalization	95, 96
Comprehension		Punctuation	98, 99
Listening	65, 66	Expression/Usage	103, 104
Pictures	67	**Math**	
Sentences	70–72	Concepts/Applications	
Stories	73–85	Patterns/Sequence/Order	131
Language		Numeration	132
Spelling	89	Geometry	142, 143
Capitalization	95, 96	Measurement	144–147
Punctuation	98, 99	Number Theory	133–137
Expression/Usage	103, 104	Problem Solving	148–153
Work–Study Skills		Computation	123–130
Maps	116	**Study Skills**	
Graphs/Tables	117	Table of Contents	120
Alphabetical Order	118, 119	Alphabetical Order	118, 119
Table of Contents	120		
Classifying	121		
Reference Materials	122		
Math Concepts/Applications			
Numeration	132		
Number Theory	133–137		
Whole Numbers	136		
Fractions/Money	138–140		
Geometry	142, 143		
Measurement	144–147		
Math Problem Solving			
Addition Problems	148, 150		
Subtraction Problems	149, 151		
Two-Step Problems	153		
Math Computation			
Addition	123, 124		
Subtraction	125, 126		

A Look at Skills Tested in MAT: Third Edition (1–3)

A Look at Skills Tested in MAT: Fourth Edition (P1 and P2)

Book 1 (P1)	Book 2 (P2)

Skill	Page	Skill	Page
Reading/Vocabulary		**Reading/Vocabulary**	
Beginning Sounds	36, 39	Word Recognition	42
Ending Sounds	37	Synonyms	58
Word Recognition	42	Antonyms	59
Synonyms	58	**Reading/Comprehension**	
Antonyms	59	Comprehension Skills	73–85
Reading/Comprehension		**Math**	
Pictures	67	Concepts/Applications	
Stories	73–85	Place Value	137
Math		Numeration	132
Concepts/Applications		Geometry	142, 143
Numeration	132	Measurement	144–147
Fractions	138	Fractions	138
Money	139, 140	Number Families	133
Problem Solving		Graphs	141
Reading Graphs	141	Problem Solving	148–153
Story Problems	148–153	Computation	
Computation		Addition	123, 124
Addition	123, 124	Subtraction	125, 126
Subtraction	125, 126	**Language**	
Language		Listening	65, 66
Listening	65, 66	Correct Sentences	107, 108
Sequence	111	Usage	103, 104
Usage	103, 104	Punctuation	100
Punctuation	100	Capitalization	93
Capitalization	93	Alphabetical Order	118, 119
Table of Contents	120	Table of Contents	120
Alphabetizing	118, 119	Spelling	89
Spelling	89		

A Look at Skills Tested in SAT: (K–3)

Primary (K–1)		Book A (1–3)	
Skill	**Page**	**Skill**	**Page**
Visual/Auditory Recognition		**Word Analysis/Attack**	
Letters	31–33	Beginning Sounds	36, 39
Letter Groups/Words	34	Ending Sounds	37, 40
Word Pairs	35	Vowel Sounds	42
Beginning Sounds	36	Inflectional Endings	50
Rhyming Sounds	38	Contractions	46
Word Analysis/Attack		Compound Words	45
Beginning Consonants	39	**Vocabulary/Words**	
Word Recognition	53	Word Reading	53
Sight Words/Vocabulary	44	Word Meanings	54
Words and Pictures	53	Context Clues	64
Vocabulary/Words		Multiple Meanings	62, 63
Categories	55–57	**Comprehension**	
Meanings	58–64	Listening	65, 66
Comprehension		Riddles	86
Listening	65, 66	Story Completion	72
Sentences	70–72	Stories	73–85
Math Computation		**Spelling**	
Addition	123, 124	Spelling Skills	90
Subtraction	125, 126	**Language**	
Math Concepts/Applications		Capitalization	94
Numeration	132	Punctuation	100
Number Concepts	133–137	Usage	103
Measurement	144–147	Sentences	109
Geometry	142, 143	Alphabetical Order	118, 119
Problem Solving	148–153	**Math Computation**	
		Addition	123, 124
		Subtraction	125, 126
		Multiplication	127, 128
		Division	129, 130
		Math Concepts/Applications	
		Numeration	132
		Number Concepts	133–137
		Problem Solving	148–153
		Measurement	144–147
		Geometry	142, 143

A Look at Skills Tested in TAAS: Grade 3

Grade 3

Skill	Page
Reading/Word Skills	
Vocabulary	64
Consonants	39, 40
Vowels	42
Word Parts	61
Reading/Comprehension	
Pictures	67
Sentences	70–72, 107, 108
Stories	73–85
Math Concepts/Applications	
Numeration	132
Geometry	142, 143
Measurement	144–147
Problem Solving	148–153
Math Operations	
Addition	123, 124
Subtraction	125, 126
Multiplication	127, 128
Division	129, 130
Language Skills	
Spelling	90
Listening	53–57, 65, 66
Punctuation	100
Usage	103, 104
Capitalization	93
Sentences	107, 108

Visual/Auditory Recognition: Letters

Samples

		e	c	u	s
		○	○	○	○
		A	**V**	**W**	**Y**
		○	○	○	○

1.		**t**	**f**	**r**	**l**
		○	○	○	○
2.		**H**	**N**	**M**	**K**
		○	○	○	○
3.		**g**	**y**	**j**	**q**
		○	○	○	○
4.		**Z**	**X**	**K**	**T**
		○	○	○	○
5.		**b**	**d**	**q**	**p**
		○	○	○	○
6.		**O**	**C**	**D**	**Q**
		○	○	○	○
7.		**s**	**e**	**o**	**a**
		○	○	○	○

Visual Auditory Recognition: Letters (Uppercase/Lowercase)

Samples

		E	e	c	u	s
			○	○	○	○
		a	A	V	W	Y
			○	○	○	○

			t	f	r	l
1.	R		○	○	○	○
2.	h		H	N	M	K
			○	○	○	○
3.	Q		g	y	j	q
			○	○	○	○
4.	t		Z	X	K	T
			○	○	○	○
5.	B		b	d	q	p
			○	○	○	○
6.	d		O	C	D	Q
			○	○	○	○
7.	A		s	e	o	a
			○	○	○	○

Visual Auditory Recognition: Letters (in Words)

Samples

	c	cat ○	man ○	old ○
	b	pot ○	tiger ○	bed ○

1.	o	can ○	cold ○	pet ○
2.	x	eat ○	fox ○	run ○
3.	n	yes ○	no ○	rug ○
4.	k	ball ○	kite ○	cot ○
5.	t	mat ○	man ○	old ○
6.	d	bear ○	bird ○	bunny ○
7.	s	sun ○	girl ○	cake ○

Visual Auditory Recognition: Letter Groups/Words

Samples

	sh	ch ○	ck ○	sh ○	st ○

	stop	spot ○	pots ○	step ○	stop ○

1.	cl	lc ○	cr ○	bl ○	cl ○
2.	FO	OFF ○	OF ○	IF ○	FO ○
3.	ng	nd ○	ny ○	np ○	ng ○
4.	like	lick ○	luck ○	like ○	look ○
5.	bat	but ○	bat ○	tab ○	bit ○
6.	now	won ○	own ○	now ○	not ○
7.	will	with ○	will ○	wig ○	wish ○
8.	top	top ○	pot ○	stop ○	pop ○

Visual Auditory Recognition: Word Pairs

Samples

○   ○

○   ○

1.

○   ○

2.

○   ○

3.

○   ○

Word Analysis/Attack: Beginning Sounds

Sample

  (cat) (dog) (egg)
○   ○   ○

1. 
○   ○   ○

2. 
○   ○   ○

3. 
○   ○   ○

4. 
○   ○   ○

5. 
○   ○   ○

6. 
○   ○   ○

Word Analysis/Attack: Ending Sounds

Sample

   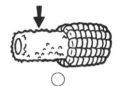

○ ○ ○

1.

○ ○ ○

2.

○ ○ ○

3.

○ ○ ○

4.

○ ○ ○

5.

○ ○ ○

6.

○ ○ ○

Word Analysis/Attack: Rhyming Sounds

Samples

  ○   ○  ○

1.  ○  ○   ○

2.  ○  ○   ○

3.  ○   ○   ○

4.   ○   ○   ○

5.  ○   ○  ○

6.   ○  ○ 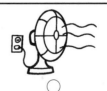 ○

Word Analysis/Attack: Beginning Consonants

Samples

	good	bell	dog	funny
	○	○	○	○

	pan	sang	cat	may
	○	○	○	○

1. | | next | from | too | bell |
| ○ | ○ | ○ | ○ |

2. | | pin | keep | make | right |
| ○ | ○ | ○ | ○ |

3. | | rug | sun | top | can |
| ○ | ○ | ○ | ○ |

4. | | fall | goat | tiger | jump |
| ○ | ○ | ○ | ○ |

5. | | truck | this | twice |
| ○ | ○ | ○ |

6. | | chalk | crayon | clap |
| ○ | ○ | ○ |

7. | | sheet | still | school |
| ○ | ○ | ○ |

Word Analysis/Attack: Ending Consonants

Samples

	cat ○	go ○	log ○	tub ○
	ce<u>nt</u> ○	ba<u>nd</u> ○	ta<u>nk</u> ○	

1.   hen ○   bread ○   night ○   cup ○

2.   green ○   blue ○   white ○   red ○

3.   pull ○   lap ○   glass ○   mug ○

4.   frie<u>nd</u> ○   ba<u>nk</u> ○   wa<u>nt</u> ○

5.   mu<u>st</u> ○   wi<u>sh</u> ○   de<u>sk</u> ○

6.   swi<u>ng</u> ○   mi<u>nd</u> ○   se<u>nt</u> ○

7.   ta<u>lk</u> ○   fe<u>lt</u> ○   he<u>lp</u> ○

Word Analysis/Attack: Consonant Substitutions

Samples

  |

○   ○   ○

__ ook | b ○   c ○   t ○

---

1. |

f ○   ○   ○

---

2. |

c ○   ○   ○

---

3. 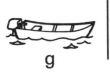 | ○   ○   ○

g

4.

__ og | l ○   b ○   d ○

5.

__ __ ing | sl ○   sw ○   st ○

6.

__ air | ch ○   th ○   sh ○

Word Analysis/Attack: Vowel Sounds

Samples

⇨ c<u>a</u>t

make ○	sand ○	draw ○

⇨ c<u>a</u>ke

bad ○	made ○	fan ○

---

1. p<u>o</u>t

boat ○	rode ○	log ○

2. m<u>e</u>t

meat ○	bed ○	see ○

3. sl<u>i</u>p

wide ○	right ○	did ○

4. m<u>a</u>p

gate ○	baby ○	happy ○

5. d<u>u</u>ck

cute ○	lunch ○	use ○

6. m<u>a</u>ke

tail ○	back ○	are ○

7. s<u>ee</u>

well ○	get ○	meat ○

8. l<u>i</u>ke

lick ○	bright ○	skin ○

9. t<u>o</u>ld

ghost ○	too ○	clock ○

10. <u>u</u>se

up ○	under ○	cute ○

11. cr<u>ow</u>n

brown ○	grown ○	throw ○

12. c<u>au</u>se

rain ○	saw ○	cake ○

13. cl<u>ow</u>n

could ○	cloud ○	low ○

14. t<u>oy</u>

coin ○	top ○	yo-yo ○

Word Analysis/Attack: Silent Letters

Samples

sword	twenty	swan
○	○	○

drop	write	word
○	○	○

1.

not	king	knee
○	○	○

2.

lamb	lamp	number
○	○	○

3.

camp	comb	car
○	○	○

4.

worm	and	answer
○	○	○

5.

knight	giant	dragon
○	○	○

6.

now	know	won
○	○	○

Word Analysis/Attack: Sight Words/Vocabulary

Samples

	toy	boy	box	bus
	○	○	○	○

	no	know	now	won
	○	○	○	○

1.	mother	other	father	bother
	○	○	○	○

2.	bake	back	book	bark
	○	○	○	○

3.	take	tack	talk	took
	○	○	○	○

4.	said	say	says	sees
	○	○	○	

5.	like	look	lack	lick
	○	○	○	○

6.	pebble	pocket	people	peep
	○	○	○	○

7.	there	were	where	wear
	○	○	○	○

Word Analysis/Attack: Compound Words

Sample

	friendly	football	balloon	beautiful
	○	○	○	○

1.	basketball	present	until	window
	○	○	○	○

2.	unhappy	feather	someone	rabbit
	○	○	○	○

3.	mother	sunny	ribbon	rainbow
	○	○	○	○

4.	snowball	money	other	answer
	○	○	○	

5.	basket	everyone	yesterday	building
	○	○	○	○

6.	careful	country	circle	cupcake
	○	○	○	○

7.	children	riding	cardboard	begin
	○	○	○	○

Word Analysis/Attack: Contractions

Sample

	is none	is not	is net	is nothing
isn't	○	○	○	○

1.	I will	I call	I tell	I fell
I'll	○	○	○	○
2.	won to	will not	won not	will let
won't	○	○	○	○
3.	let see	let go	let us	let in
let's	○	○	○	○
4.	you are	you have	you care	you dare
you're	○	○	○	○
5.	I come	I came	I	I am
I'm	○	○	○	○
6.	can at	can sit	can not	can to
can't	○	○	○	○
7.	he has	he is	he was	he his
he's	○	○	○	○

Word Analysis/Attack: Root Words

Samples

	un	hap	happy	unhap
unhappy	○	○	○	○

	slow	est	west	slo
slowest	○	○	○	○

1.	ly	ickly	quick	ick
quickly	○	○	○	○
2.	un	fair	fai	air
unfair	○	○	○	○
3.	cook	ing	ook	king
cooking	○	○	○	○
4.	re	pa	rep	pay
repay	○	○	○	○
5.	pain	paint	aint	er
painter	○	○	○	○
6.	re	ret	turn	urn
return	○	○	○	○
7.	friend	rien	end	ly
friendly	○	○	○	○

Word Analysis/Attack: Prefixes

Sample

	un	under	ground	round
underground	○	○	○	○

1.	over	ov	he	head
overhead	○	○	○	○

2.	u	un	unhap	happy
unhappy	○	○	○	○

3.	dis	dish	hon	est
dishonest	○	○	○	○

4.	un	under	erl	line
underline	○	○	○	○

5.	un	was	wash	washed
unwashed	○	○	○	○

6.	di	dis	lik	like
dislike	○	○	○	○

7.	re	ret	tu	turn
return	○	○	○	○

Word Analysis/Attack: Suffixes

Sample

	cer	ly	tain	tainly
certainly	○	○	○	○

1.	use	sef	ful	ul
useful	○	○	○	○
2.	real	all	lly	ly
really	○	○	○	○
3.	slow	low	wer	er
slower	○	○	○	○
4.	fast	test	est	st
fastest	○	○	○	○
5.	won	wonder	derful	ful
wonderful	○	○	○	○
6.	friend	end	dly	ly
friendly	○	○	○	○
7.	baby	bab	yish	ish
babyish	○	○	○	○

Word Analysis/Attack: Inflectional Endings

Samples

A.

- ○ walk
- ○ walking
- ○ walks

B.

- ○ brighter
- ○ brightest
- ○ brightly

1.

- ○ runner
- ○ running
- ○ runs

5.

- ○ hops
- ○ hopped
- ○ hopping

2.

- ○ nicer
- ○ nicest
- ○ nicely

6.

- ○ neatly
- ○ neater
- ○ neatest

3.

- ○ painter
- ○ painted
- ○ painting

7.

- ○ mailing
- ○ mailed
- ○ mails

4.

- ○ happily
- ○ happier
- ○ happiest

8.

- ○ shouting
- ○ shouted
- ○ shouts

Word Analysis/Attack: Syllables

Sample

	1	2	3	4
beautiful	○	○	○	○

1.	1	2	3	4
transportation	○	○	○	○

2.	1	2	3	4
alive	○	○	○	○

3.	1	2	3	4
anybody	○	○	○	○

4.	1	2	3	4
chalk	○	○	○	○

5.	1	2	3	4
picture	○	○	○	○

6.	1	2	3	4
exciting	○	○	○	○

7.	1	2	3	4
library	○	○	○	○

Word Analysis/Attack: Endings/Compounds

Samples

A.

walk	est	ly	ing
	○	○	○

B.

foot	all	care
ball	most	full
○	○	○

1.

trust	ed	ly	ness
	○	○	○

5.

real	side	doll
lea	walk	are
○	○	○

2.

danger	ly	ous	ful
	○	○	○

6.

mark	bum	out
ker	bull	doors
○	○	○

3.

forget	ly	ment	ful
	○	○	○

7.

play	hi	beauty
ground	way	full
○	○	○

4.

friend	ship	ing	ness
	○	○	○

8.

day	car	any
shunt	tune	one
○	○	○

Vocabulary: Pictures (1)

Sample

	goat	girl	good	go
	○	○	○	○

1. | horse | house | heart | happy |
   | ○ | ○ | ○ | ○ |

2. | back | box | book | bake |
   | ○ | ○ | ○ | ○ |

3. | ball | bell | bull | balloon |
   | ○ | ○ | ○ | ○ |

4. | crown | clown | cloud | crowd |
   | ○ | ○ | ○ | |

5. | car | everyone | yesterday | building |
   | ○ | ○ | ○ | ○ |

6. | careful | cat | cap | car |
   | ○ | ○ | ○ | ○ |

7. | clock | cloak | claw | kick |
   | ○ | ○ | ○ | ○ |

Vocabulary: Pictures (2)

Sample

○   ○   ○

1.

○   ○   ○

2.

○   ○   ○

3.

○   ○   ○

4.

○   ○   ○

Vocabulary: Word Categories

Sample

1.

2.

3.

4.

5.

6.

Vocabulary: Word Categories (and Meanings)

Samples

	happy	rainy	angry	funny
	○	○	○	○
	walk	hop	run	stand
	○	○	○	○

1. | lion | cat | cow | moose |
   | ○ | ○ | ○ | ○ |

2. | breakfast | milk | carrot | fruit |
   | ○ | ○ | ○ | ○ |

3. | day | sun | sky | cloud |
   | ○ | ○ | ○ | ○ |

4. | tree | oak | pine | rose |
   | ○ | ○ | ○ | ○ |

5. | library | bank | hospital | store |
   | ○ | ○ | ○ | ○ |

6. | sidewalk | street | crossing | signal |
   | ○ | ○ | ○ | ○ |

7. | short | far | slow | wide |
   | ○ | ○ | ○ | ○ |

Vocabulary: Word Categories (Does Not Belong)

Sample

	ball	bat	mitt	carrot
	○	○	○	○

1.	uncle	aunt	mother	doctor
	○	○	○	○

2.	up	dirty	down	under
	○	○	○	○

3.	read	run	walk	hop
	○	○	○	○

4.	milk	juice	bread	water
	○	○	○	○

5.	house	car	bus	taxi
	○	○	○	○

6.	day	month	year	when
	○	○	○	○

7.	tulip	rose	dog	daisy
	○	○	○	○

Vocabulary: Words with Similar Meanings

Samples

A. large glass of milk

- ○ small
- ○ big
- ○ cold

B. bake a cake

- ○ decorate
- ○ ice
- ○ cook

1. frighten her

- ○ scare
- ○ surprise
- ○ ask

5. finish the race

- ○ start
- ○ end
- ○ watch

2. pretty picture

- ○ another
- ○ colorful
- ○ beautiful

6. ran fast

- ○ quickly
- ○ slow
- ○ hard

3. his mother

- ○ pet
- ○ friend
- ○ mom

7. in the town

- ○ city
- ○ country
- ○ desert

4. tall building

- ○ high
- ○ low
- ○ new

8. in a heap

- ○ mess
- ○ basket
- ○ pile

Vocabulary: Words with Opposite Meanings

Samples

A.   a <u>hot</u> room

    ○ warm

    ○ crowded

    ○ cold

B.   <u>end</u> the story

    ○ finish

    ○ begin

    ○ stop

1.   a <u>sick</u> child

    ○ healthy

    ○ ill

    ○ injured

5.   a <u>happy</u> story

    ○ funny

    ○ pleasant

    ○ sad

2.   <u>dry</u> weather

    ○ cold

    ○ chilly

    ○ humid

6.   a <u>noisy</u> room

    ○ loud

    ○ quiet

    ○ busy

3.   a <u>long</u> time

    ○ boring

    ○ short

    ○ lengthy

7.   the <u>beautiful</u> lion

    ○ ugly

    ○ strong

    ○ handsome

4.   <u>wreck</u> the building

    ○ build

    ○ ruin

    ○ destroy

8.   a <u>hard</u> test

    ○ difficult

    ○ easy

    ○ long

Vocabulary: Suffix Meanings

Samples

A. Washington<u>ian</u> Houston<u>ian</u>

- ○ state of
- ○ person from
- ○ place for

B. guitar<u>ist</u> pian<u>ist</u>

- ○ place for
- ○ person who
- ○ state of being

1. work<u>er</u> paint<u>er</u>

- ○ place for
- ○ one who
- ○ able to be

5. happi<u>ness</u> sad<u>ness</u>

- ○ person who
- ○ state of being
- ○ place for

2. small<u>ish</u> green<u>ish</u>

- ○ somewhat
- ○ able to be
- ○ most

6. discover<u>able</u> spend<u>able</u>

- ○ not yet able
- ○ not able
- ○ able to be

3. bigg<u>est</u> tini<u>est</u>

- ○ more
- ○ most
- ○ rather

7. transporta<u>tion</u> communica<u>tion</u>

- ○ able to be
- ○ the person who
- ○ the act of

4. high<u>er</u> low<u>er</u>

- ○ more
- ○ most
- ○ rather

8. lat<u>er</u> slow<u>er</u>

- ○ rather
- ○ more
- ○ most

Vocabulary: Word Part Clues

Samples

A. She was _____ because she broke her toy.

- ○ nonhappy
- ○ imhappy
- ○ mishappy
- ○ unhappy

B. Carla is _____ a book.

- ○ reads
- ○ reading
- ○ read
- ○ ready

1. The boy _____ the tree yesterday.

- ○ climbed
- ○ climber
- ○ climb
- ○ climbs

4. My seat is in the _____ row.

- ○ fours
- ○ forty
- ○ four
- ○ fourth

2. Mindy used a new tape to _____ the speech.

- ○ precord
- ○ transcord
- ○ record
- ○ discord

5. Mrs. Taylor taught her class some _____ rules.

- ○ saver
- ○ savings
- ○ safety
- ○ safely

3. Get your brakes _____ before you ride your bike.

- ○ repaired
- ○ impaired
- ○ depaired
- ○ subpaired

6. John needs help to _____ that box.

- ○ opening
- ○ open
- ○ opener
- ○ opens

Vocabulary: Multiple Meanings (Definitions)

Sample

something to wear and short, quick breaths

○ shirts   ○ trousers   ○ shouts   ○ pants

1.   a path and to follow

○ road   ○ trail   ○ copy   ○ lead

2.   increase in pay and lift up

○ raise   ○ money   ○ elevator   ○ more

3.   an animal sound and a tree's covering

○ growl   ○ branch   ○ bark   ○ leaf

4.   a street number and to speak to

○ address   ○ say   ○ voice   ○ place

5.   to have seen and to cut with a tool

○ chop   ○ saw   ○ see   ○ watch

Vocabulary: Multiple Meanings (in Sentences)

Sample

They did not play_____.

We rode the ferris wheel at the _____.

     ○ well   ○ carnival   ○ fair   ○ long

---

1. Do you have time to _____me practice?

    My _____is not keeping time.

     ○ watch   ○ clock   ○ see   ○ observe

---

2. Jerry ripped his _____ on the slide.

    My dog _____ when she is hot.

     ○ shirt   ○ pants   ○ sleep   ○ drinks

---

3. Maria cannot find socks to _____ her dress.

    Do not burn yourself with that _____.

     ○ candle   ○ suit   ○ match   ○ fire

---

4. We have tickets to see the _____.

    Can you _____ with me after school?

     ○ game   ○ come   ○ concert   ○ play

---

5. Mother _____ the coffee beans in the grinder.

    The _____ is soaked from the rain.

     ○ ground   ○ put   ○ earth   ○ grass

Vocabulary: Words in Context

Samples

A. The play was very long. The actors were_____.

- ○ rested
- ○ tired
- ○ glad
- ○ ready

B. Our cat was missing. We _____ her name until she came home.

- ○ called
- ○ wrote
- ○ wished
- ○ whispered

1. The puddle was too big to jump over. We had to _____ around it.

- ○ stand
- ○ look
- ○ carry
- ○ walk

2. Yesterday I helped Dad paint the _____ around our yard.

- ○ floor
- ○ fence
- ○ trees
- ○ nest

The playground was ___(3)___ . All of the classes went to ___(4)___ at the same time.

3.
- ○ empty
- ○ crowded
- ○ big
- ○ small

4.
- ○ recess
- ○ school
- ○ study
- ○ science

Our classroom has ___(5)___ shelves. We use a ladder to reach the books on the ___(6)___ .

5.
- ○ low
- ○ long
- ○ tall
- ○ many

6.
- ○ bottom
- ○ top
- ○ sides
- ○ ends

Reading Comprehension: Listening (Sentences)

Sample

   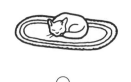

○ ○ ○

1.

○ ○ ○

2.

○ ○ ○

3.

○ ○ ○

4.

○ ○ ○

5.

○ ○ ○

Reading Comprehension: Listening (Stories)

Sample

○ ○ ○

1.

○ ○ ○

2.

 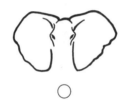 

○ ○ ○

3.

 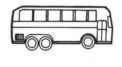 

○ ○ ○

4.

○ ○ ○

5.

○ ○ ○

Reading Comprehension: Sentences (1 Picture/3 Sentences)

Sample

○ This is a piece of wood.

○ The board has a hole in it.

○ The hole is round.

1.

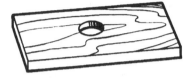

○ Gil and Sarah are at the zoo.

○ Monkeys like to eat bananas.

○ We went to the park.

2.

○ The boys would like to buy a train.

○ The boys are playing with the train.

○ The train track is on the floor.

3.

○ There is a hole in the wall.

○ The mouse ate all of the cheese.

○ The mouse is going back to his hole.

4.

○ There are many books here.

○ The girl is at the library.

○ A girl is reading a book.

Reading Comprehension: Word Recognition

Samples

A.

like	look	light
○	○	○

B.

one	oh	out
○	○	○

1.

shoe	show	slow
○	○	○

8.

many	baby	body
○	○	○

2.

blue	blow	black
○	○	○

9.

pretty	pretend	present
○	○	○

3.

spot	stop	pots
○	○	○

10.

of	off	for
○	○	○

4.

know	now	no
○	○	○

11.

can	came	come
○	○	○

5.

were	where	wore
○	○	○

12.

smile	smell	sniff
○	○	○

6.

along	able	alone
○	○	○

13.

run	ran	rain
○	○	○

7.

clown	crown	crumb
○	○	○

14.

happy	funny	baby
○	○	○

Reading Comprehension: Word Attack

Samples

A. Pat is wearing a new hat.

○   ○   ○

B. My cat likes to play. Her favorite toy is a stuffed mouse.

○   ○   ○

1. We went to the baseball game. Dad bought me some peanuts.

○   ○   ○

4. The boys enjoyed recess. Ken played baseball.

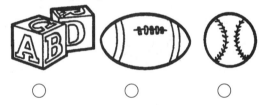

○   ○   ○

2. Fred asked, "May I sail your boat?"

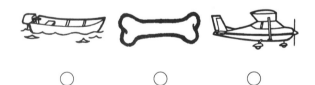

○   ○   ○

5. Jan put her hands out when she fell. She hurt her finger.

○   ○   ○

3. Where did the mouse go? It went behind the stove.

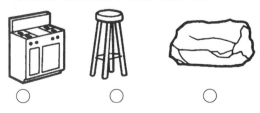

○   ○   ○

6. Myra went to the party. She wore a pretty dress.

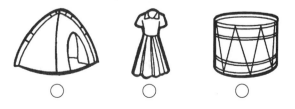

○   ○   ○

Reading Comprehension: Sentences (1 Sentence/3 Pictures)

Sample

 The man is feeding the dog.

1. The fence is around the house.

2. The kittens are playing.

3. The girl is riding a bike.

4. The boys are eating ice cream cones.

5. The teacher is holding a globe.

Reading Comprehension: Sentences (1 Picture/3 Sentences)

Sample

○ The boy is reading a book.

○ The girl can jump rope.

○ The boy is bouncing the ball.

1.

○ All the children are reading.

○ No one is sitting on the bench.

○ Two children are jumping rope.

2.

○ "Lunch is ready," Mother calls.

○ "Where is the dog?" Mother asks.

○ "Here is some pizza," Mother says.

3.

○ They are running down the stairs.

○ They are running up the stairs.

○ They are sitting on the stairs.

4.

○ They are playing in the water.

○ They are playing in the sand.

○ They are sitting under the umbrella.

Reading Comprehension: Sentences (with Blanks)

Sample

The train is on the _____.

road	track	water	runway
○	○	○	○

1. John turned the _____ on.

door	desk	light	wall
○	○	○	○

2. This sandwich is _____.

good	far	up	slow
○	○	○	○

3. My kitten _____ to play.

is	was	looks	likes
○	○	○	○

4. Mother _____ us for dinner.

said	called	sang	says
○	○	○	○

5. "Please fill the _____ with water," said Mother.

plates	boxes	glasses	spoons
○	○	○	○

Reading Comprehension: Stories

Story Sample

Dinosaurs lived all over the Earth many millions of years ago. Some of them were very big. Others were no larger than a chicken. Some of them ate plants. Some of them ate other dinosaurs. The ones that ate other dinosaurs were called <u>carnivores</u>. Scientists learn about dinosaurs from their bones. You can see these bones in many museums.

1. What is the story mainly about?

   ○ chickens

   ○ plant eaters

   ○ bones

   ○ dinosaurs

2. How do scientists learn about dinosaurs?

   ○ from their bones

   ○ from museums

   ○ by looking at plants

   ○ by studying chickens

3. Is this story about things that really happened?

   ○ Yes

   ○ No

4. In this story, <u>carnivores</u> means

   ○ dinosaurs.

   ○ plant eaters.

   ○ meat eaters.

   ○ scientists.

Reading Comprehension: Stories

Story 1, Page 1

🌳 Mary, Sally, and their mom and dad had been planning their summer vacation for many months. They were going to take a trip to Disney World in Florida. Then things started to go wrong. The car needed to be repaired. Mom lost her job. Dad fell down at work and broke his arm.

"I'm sorry, kids," Dad said. "I guess we will have to go to Disney World next year."

1. Why did the family need to put off their trip?
   - ○ Dad changed his mind.
   - ○ It was not summer yet.
   - ○ Things started to go wrong.
   - ○ They needed a new car.

2. How do you think Mary and Sally felt?
   - ○ happy
   - ○ sad
   - ○ excited
   - ○ mean

3. What do you think the family will do now?
   - ○ keep planning
   - ○ give up
   - ○ go somewhere else
   - ○ become angry

4. In this story, repaired means . . .
   - ○ replaced.
   - ○ repainted.
   - ○ serviced.
   - ○ fixed.

Reading Comprehension: Stories

Story 1, Page 2

Mary and Sally spent the first day of their vacation cleaning up the yard and setting up their small pool. They got out all of the pool toys. The sandbox needed new sand, but they got out the sand toys anyway. Then they wiped off the table and chairs. After a long search, they found their picnic things in the garage. The girls were <u>preparing</u> to have a wonderful summer.

5. What is the main idea of this part of the story?
    ○ The girls were preparing to have a wonderful summer.
    ○ The girls were bored and had nothing to do.
    ○ The yard was a terrible mess.
    ○ All of the toys were in the garage.

6. Where did the girls find their picnic things?
    ○ in the pool
    ○ in the sandbox
    ○ in the garage
    ○ in the yard

7. What did the girls do after they got out the sand toys?
    ○ They cleaned up the yard.
    ○ They wiped off the table and chairs.
    ○ They set up the pool.
    ○ They got out the pool toys.

8. In this story, <u>preparing</u> means . . .
    ○ working.
    ○ playing.
    ○ going away.
    ○ getting ready.

Reading Comprehension: Stories

Story 1, Page 3

"This looks like fun," said Mom, looking around the yard at what the girls had done. "And I have some good news for you. We are going to be able to go to Disney World after all! Then, when we <u>return</u>, you can enjoy your pool and sandbox for the rest of the summer."

Sally and Mary danced around the yard. This really was going to be a wonderful summer!

---

9. What do you think must have happened?

   ○ More things went wrong.

   ○ Things started to get better.

   ○ Mary and Sally were having fun.

   ○ Mary and Sally were feeling sad.

---

10. What might be a good title for this story?

    ○ A Sad Time

    ○ A Busy Time

    ○ Mom's Secret

    ○ The Happy Ending

---

11. Is this story about things that could really happen?

    ○ Yes

    ○ No

---

12. In this story, <u>return</u> means . . .

    ○ take back.

    ○ come back.

    ○ recycle.

    ○ turn around.

STOP

Reading Comprehension: Stories

Story 2, Page 1

Elmer Elf sat under his toadstool and watched the rain pour down around him. His feet, in their pointed green shoes, were <u>soggy</u> and cold. Having wet feet made Elmer sneeze.

"Rats!" said Elmer. "I wish this rain would stop. I want to do something fun."

Suddenly, a rainbow appeared in the sky.

1. What made Elmer sneeze?
   ○ being cold
   ○ having wet feet
   ○ sitting under a toadstool
   ○ wearing green shoes

2. How did Elmer feel?
   ○ happy
   ○ sad
   ○ excited
   ○ cross

3. What do you think will happen next?
   ○ Elmer will go to sleep.
   ○ Elmer will watch the rain.
   ○ It will keep raining.
   ○ The rain will stop.

4. In this story, <u>soggy</u> means . . .
   ○ really wet.
   ○ really cold.
   ○ pointed.
   ○ dirty.

Reading Comprehension: Stories

Story 2, Page 2

🌳 When the rain stopped, Elmer <u>crept</u> out from under the toadstool. He took off his shoes and put them on top of the toadstool to dry in the sun.

While he waited for his shoes to dry, Elmer sat on a rock and sang a song just because he was so happy. He decided to go to visit his friend Oswald Owl at his home in a hollow tree. He thought maybe they could have dinner together.

---

5. What is the main idea of this part of the story?
- ○ Elmer was happy because the rain stopped.
- ○ Elmer's shoes took a long time to dry.
- ○ Elmer made up a happy song.
- ○ One of Elmer's friends is an owl.

6. What did Elmer do first after the rain stopped?
- ○ crept out from under the toadstool
- ○ took off his shoes
- ○ laid his shoes out to dry
- ○ sang a happy song

7. Where did Elmer put his shoes to dry?
- ○ under the toadstool
- ○ on top of the toadstool
- ○ on a rock
- ○ in a hollow tree

8. In this story, <u>crept</u> means . . .
- ○ crawled.
- ○ sneaked.
- ○ walked.
- ○ swam.

Reading Comprehension: Stories

Story 2, Page 3

As soon as his shoes were dry, Elmer put them back on and set off for Oswald Owl's hollow tree.

"Hi, Elmer," hooted Oswald. "<u>Enter</u>! I was just thinking about you. How about some dinner?"

"Oh, thank you," said Elmer. "I was hoping to do something that would be fun."

After dinner, Elmer and Oswald played games. They had a good time.

---

9. What did you notice about Oswald?

○ He wanted to be alone.

○ He was very hungry.

○ He did not like Elmer.

○ He was glad to see Elmer.

---

10. What might be a good title for this story?

○ Oswald's Day

○ Elmer's Day

○ Elmer's Shoes

○ A Rainy Day

---

11. Is this story about things that could really happen?

○ Yes

○ No

---

12. In this story, <u>enter</u> means . . .

○ go away.

○ leave.

○ come back.

○ come in.

STOP

Reading Comprehension: Stories

Story 3, Page 1

Zoos today are much nicer than they used to be. In old-fashioned zoos the animals were kept alone in small cages that were sometimes dirty. Often they became sick because they were not <u>protected from</u> the weather. They had no room to run around. Modern zoos keep animals in large places that look like their real homes. They live with other animals like they would in the wild.

1. What reason does the story give for why animals often became sick in old-fashioned zoos?
    - They were kept alone in small cages.
    - Their cages were often dirty.
    - They were not protected from the weather.
    - They did not have room to run around.

2. How did the animals in old-fashioned zoos probably feel?
    - happy
    - lonely
    - excited
    - cross

3. What would happen if animals were put back in old-fashioned zoos today?
    - They might get sick.
    - They might like it.
    - They might have clean cages.
    - They might be glad to sit still.

4. In this story, <u>protected from</u> means . . .
    - used to.
    - able to feel.
    - kept out in.
    - kept safe from.

Reading Comprehension: Stories

Story 3, Page 2

Animals are kept in zoos for several reasons. Sometimes they are kept in zoos when there is not enough room for them anymore. This happens when people need to use the land the animals are living on. They are sometimes kept in zoos to protect them from hunters. Some people hunt wild animals for their skins and their ivory. Animals are also kept in zoos so that people can see them without traveling to <u>distant</u> places. When unusual animals are brought to zoos, people often line up to look at them.

5. What is the main idea of this part of the story?
   ○ Animals are kept in zoos for several reasons.
   ○ Animals are kept in zoos to protect them from hunters.
   ○ Animals are kept in zoos when people need to use their homelands.
   ○ Animals are kept in zoos so that people can look at them.

6. What happens after unusual animals are brought to zoos?
   ○ People quickly forget about them.
   ○ People can hunt them easily.
   ○ People can take the animals' lands.
   ○ Many people come to see them.

7. What is one thing that makes people want to hunt wild animals?
   ○ ivory
   ○ land
   ○ zoos
   ○ guns

8. In this story, <u>distant</u> means . . .
   ○ nearby.
   ○ far away.
   ○ interesting.
   ○ dangerous.

Reading Comprehension: Stories

Story 3, Page 3

When people visit zoos to look at the animals, they often go to see their favorite ones. Some people like the biggest ones the best. They like to see the elephants, rhinoceroses, and giraffes. Some people like to visit the snake houses. They like the boa constrictors, the anacondas, and the rattlesnakes. Other people are interested in the monkeys and the apes. The baboons, chimpanzees, and gorillas are their favorites. Finally, there are the people who like all of the animals. They try to see the entire zoo!

9. According to this story, what can you tell about people who go to the zoo?

   ○ They all want to see the elephants.

   ○ They all like to look at the snakes.

   ○ They are all interested in apes and monkeys.

   ○ They are interested in different things.

10. What might be a good title for this story?

    ○ People at the Zoo

    ○ Animals in the Wild

    ○ The Snake House

    ○ Apes and Monkeys

11. Is this story about things that are real?

    ○ Yes

    ○ No

12. In this story, entire means . . .

    ○ interesting.

    ○ whole.

    ○ favorite.

    ○ empty.

STOP

Reading Comprehension: Stories

Story 4, Page 1

Once upon a time there was a boy named Troy. He lived deep in the woods with his old grandmother. Since they were very poor, Troy did not have nice clothes to wear and sometimes he was hungry. One day while he was picking wild berries in the woods, he found an old metal <u>platter</u> under a tree. "I'll shine this up and take it home to Grandmother," he said to himself. As he rubbed the platter with the end of his ragged shirt, he thought about good things to eat. All of a sudden . . .

1. Why was Troy wearing a ragged shirt?

    ○ He lived in the woods.

    ○ He was very poor.

    ○ His grandmother was old.

    ○ He was picking berries.

2. According to the story, Troy felt . . .

    ○ happy.

    ○ lonely.

    ○ hungry.

    ○ cross.

3. What do you think will happen next?

    ○ something magical

    ○ something scary

    ○ something funny

    ○ nothing at all

4. In this story, <u>platter</u> means . . .

    ○ a bowl.

    ○ a large plate.

    ○ a treasure.

    ○ a coin.

Reading Comprehension: Stories

Story 4, Page 2

Troy was rubbing the platter with his shirt and thinking about a large sandwich when, all of a sudden, the sandwich was there on the platter. Being a <u>sensible</u> boy, he sat right down and ate it. Since the sandwich had tasted very good, Troy thought about a piece of chocolate cake just to see what would happen. The chocolate cake appeared, so he ate that too, along with the glass of milk he quickly thought of. Finally, since he was not hungry anymore, Troy started to walk home to show his grandmother what he had found.

---

5. What is the main idea of this part of the story?
   - ○ Troy made food appear on the magic platter.
   - ○ Troy thought that the sandwich tasted good.
   - ○ Troy wanted milk to go with the cake.
   - ○ Troy started to walk home to show the platter to his grandmother.

---

6. Which food appeared first on the platter?
   - ○ a sandwich
   - ○ chocolate cake
   - ○ a glass of milk
   - ○ some berries

---

7. What did Troy do with the sandwich?
   - ○ He saved it.
   - ○ He buried it.
   - ○ He ate it.
   - ○ He took it home.

---

8. In this story, <u>sensible</u> means . . .
   - ○ curious.
   - ○ smart.
   - ○ selfish.
   - ○ mean.

Reading Comprehension: Stories

Story 4, Page 3

"Grandmother! Grandmother!" Troy called as he ran into the house, "Look what I <u>discovered</u> in the woods!"

Troy asked his grandmother to sit down and think of a cup of tea while he rubbed the platter. Then they thought about cookies, and they ate them. Finally, taking a deep breath, Troy thought of money. There, on the platter, was a pile of coins.

Troy and his grandmother hugged each other. They laughed and they cried. Then they lived happily ever after.

---

9.   According to this story, the platter could probably . . .

   ○ make anything appear.

   ○ make only food appear.

   ○ make only a cake appear.

   ○ make only money appear.

---

10.   What might be a good title for this story?

   ○ Troy and His Grandmother

   ○ The House in the Forest

   ○ The Berry-Picking Day

   ○ The Magic Platter

---

11.   Could the things in this story really happen?

   ○ Yes

   ○ No

---

12.   In this story, <u>discovered</u> means . . .

   ○ lost.

   ○ found.

   ○ dug up.

   ○ polished.

STOP

Reading Comprehension: Riddles

Sample

I have legs.

I am alive.

○   ○   ○

1.

I can spin.

I have eight legs.

○   ○   ○

2.

It has rocks.

It is not alive.

○   ○   ○

3.

It has wings.

It can sing.

○   ○   ○

4.

It is a circle.

It goes on your hand.

○   ○   ○

5.

You can drink from me.

I am not a cup.

○   ○   ○

Spelling Skills (CAT/CTBS)

Samples

A.

That____is singing.
- ○ brd
- ○ burd
- ○ brid
- ○ bird

B.

Let's____for the train.
- ○ watsh
- ○ wach
- ○ watch
- ○ wacth

1.

His____flew away.
- ○ balloon
- ○ baloon
- ○ balune
- ○ balloone

5.

He likes to____people.
- ○ skare
- ○ scare
- ○ scear
- ○ scair

2.

Our first game is next____.
- ○ Wenesday
- ○ Wednesday
- ○ Wensday
- ○ Wendesday

6.

Don't forget your____books.
- ○ liberry
- ○ libary
- ○ libarry
- ○ library

3.

We____at all the jokes.
- ○ laffed
- ○ laghed
- ○ laughed
- ○ lafghed

7.

We have____children in our group.
- ○ ate
- ○ eight
- ○ eigth
- ○ iegth

4.

My____is coming over to play.
- ○ friend
- ○ freind
- ○ frend
- ○ freaned

8.

A chocolate cookie was my____choice.
- ○ frist
- ○ furst
- ○ first
- ○ frst

Spelling Skills (MAT/Book 2)

Samples

A. A <u>loud</u> <u>noyse</u> scared the <u>kitten</u>.
    ○   ○   ○

B. <u>Eight</u> <u>childern</u> were in the <u>classroom</u>.
    ○   ○   ○

---

1. <u>Two</u> boys are <u>absint</u> <u>today</u>.
   ○   ○   ○

2. <u>How</u> <u>many</u> <u>cookys</u> did you eat?
   ○   ○   ○

3. Bella <u>fownd</u> a <u>large</u> <u>frog</u>.
    ○   ○   ○

4. My <u>brithday</u> is <u>next</u> <u>month</u>.
    ○   ○   ○

5. The <u>book</u> is <u>too</u> high for me to <u>reatch</u>.
    ○   ○   ○

6. Move the <u>ladder</u> <u>against</u> the <u>wawl</u>.
    ○   ○   ○

7. She has a <u>prety</u> <u>new</u> <u>dress</u>.
    ○   ○   ○

8. <u>Wat</u> time <u>does</u> <u>school</u> start?
   ○   ○   ○

9. Did he <u>want</u> to <u>shair</u> his <u>candy</u>?
    ○   ○   ○

10. <u>They</u> <u>drove</u> to the zoo to see the <u>aminals</u>.
    ○   ○   ○

Spelling Skills (MAT/Book 1 and ITBS/Book A)

Samples

A.
- ○ now
- ○ jump
- ○ rope

B.
- ○ gave
- ○ candie
- ○ mother

1.
- ○ large
- ○ glass
- ○ watter

6.
- ○ cold
- ○ windy
- ○ nite

2.
- ○ Please
- ○ untill
- ○ finish

7.
- ○ Where
- ○ putt
- ○ money

3.
- ○ walks
- ○ skool
- ○ every

8.
- ○ polar
- ○ bear
- ○ wite

4.
- ○ famly
- ○ going
- ○ move

9.
- ○ leavs
- ○ trees
- ○ brown

5.
- ○ going
- ○ lunch
- ○ nune

10.
- ○ always
- ○ trie
- ○ again

Spelling Skills (MAT/Book A, SAT/Book A, and TAAS)

Samples

A.
- ○ mayk
- ○ maik
- ○ mayke
- ○ make

B.
- ○ pet
- ○ pit
- ○ pett
- ○ pete

1.
- ○ woll
- ○ wawl
- ○ waul
- ○ wall

6.
- ○ kepe
- ○ keep
- ○ keip
- ○ kepp

2.
- ○ wich
- ○ wesh
- ○ wiss
- ○ wish

7.
- ○ ranche
- ○ rantch
- ○ ransh
- ○ ranch

3.
- ○ stopp
- ○ stop
- ○ stap
- ○ stopt

8.
- ○ gamme
- ○ gaym
- ○ game
- ○ gaim

4.
- ○ maybie
- ○ mabby
- ○ maybe
- ○ maybi

9.
- ○ walking
- ○ wauking
- ○ wawking
- ○ waking

5.
- ○ lam
- ○ lamm
- ○ laam
- ○ lamb

10.
- ○ verry
- ○ vry
- ○ viry
- ○ very

Spelling Skills (SAT/Book A)

Samples

A.
- ○ animals
- ○ barn
- ○ baloon
- ○ curly

B.
- ○ childern
- ○ desk
- ○ chair
- ○ teacher

1.
- ○ cough
- ○ deer
- ○ feild
- ○ isn't

6.
- ○ agenst
- ○ loud
- ○ minute
- ○ rooster

2.
- ○ finish
- ○ laff
- ○ judge
- ○ hurry

7.
- ○ honor
- ○ baby
- ○ kichen
- ○ groceries

3.
- ○ funny
- ○ hevvy
- ○ story
- ○ taught

8.
- ○ tower
- ○ traffic
- ○ whisle
- ○ yellow

4.
- ○ Toosday
- ○ Wednesday
- ○ Thursday
- ○ Friday

9.
- ○ pretty
- ○ noyse
- ○ ticket
- ○ until

5.
- ○ notice
- ○ seven
- ○ peeple
- ○ comb

10.
- ○ pail
- ○ penny
- ○ shovle
- ○ known

Spelling Skills (ITBS/Book 2)

Samples

A.

mother   visit   munth
○   ○   ○

B.

best   suject   math
○   ○   ○

1.

watch   game   nigt
○   ○   ○

5.

truck   parked   strete
○   ○   ○

2.

thay   lunch   o'clock
○   ○   ○

6.

study   together   scool
○   ○   ○

3.

large   airplane   hous
○   ○   ○

7.

wanted   trade   cookys
○   ○   ○

4.

botom   fell   sack
○   ○   ○

8.

mother   bakeing   dinner
○   ○   ○

Language Mechanics: Capitalization (CAT/CTBS/MAT/TAAS)

Samples

A.

In september   /   we go   /   back to school.   none
   ○   ○   ○   ○

B.

The train   /   flashed by   /   on the track.   none
   ○   ○   ○   ○

1.

That dog   /   belongs to   /   ms. Baker.   none
   ○   ○   ○   ○

2.

the mail   /   was delivered   /   early today.   none
   ○   ○   ○   ○

3.

They said   /   his name is   /   dr. Murphy.   none
   ○   ○   ○   ○

4.

Spring vacation   /   is in march   /   this year.   none
   ○   ○   ○   ○

Language Mechanics: Capitalization (SAT)

Samples

A.

- ○ airplanes
- ○ very
- ○ noisy

B.

- ○ asked
- ○ mary
- ○ water

1.

- ○ i
- ○ like
- ○ ball

4.

- ○ birthday
- ○ card
- ○ uncle

2.

- ○ basketball
- ○ tuesday
- ○ evening

5.

- ○ whitewater
- ○ rafting
- ○ river

3.

- ○ when
- ○ party
- ○ start

6.

- ○ miss
- ○ homeroom
- ○ teacher

Language Mechanics: Capitalization (ITBS)

Samples

A.

- ○ My mother and I went
- ○ shopping yesterday. today
- ○ she will take my sister.

B.

- ○ Many people vacation in
- ○ California. They like to go
- ○ to disneyland.

1.

- ○ It snowed in Hawaii last
- ○ week. They seldom get snow,
- ○ even in february.

5.

- ○ Kelly's birthday is on
- ○ Saint Patrick's Day. She is
- ○ irish.

2.

- ○ Jimmy and i went to the
- ○ movies last night. We had
- ○ great popcorn.

6.

- ○ My little sister likes to
- ○ watch barney. He used to be
- ○ my favorite too.

3.

- ○ Our school is named after
- ○ President Lincoln. It is on
- ○ main Street near the park.

7.

- ○ A woman named mrs. Brown
- ○ just moved in next door. We
- ○ made some cookies for her.

4.

- ○ My favorite basketball team
- ○ is the Los Angeles lakers. Who
- ○ is your favorite team?

8.

- ○ What is the name of your
- ○ favorite book? Mine is called
- ○ *matilda* by Roald Dahl.

Language Mechanics: Capitalization (ITBS)

Samples

A. his older sister's birthday
○   ○

B. is in june.
○

C. We read *little women* in
○   ○

D. school last year.
○

---

1.   Last sunday i visited my
○   ○

2. aunt and uncle in St. louis.
○

3. We saw a play called *The cay*,
○

4. and we went to a museum. the
○

5. thing I liked most was seeing
○

6. the arch. We rode to the top of
○

7. it. I brought back a model of
○

8. a mississippi riverboat. I
○   ○

9. hope I can go back during my
○

10. next vacation. It was fun.
○

11. dear marcie,
○   ○

12.   My girl Scout troop is
○

13. selling cookies again this
○

14. year. i told our leader,
○   ○

15. mrs. watson, that you were
○   ○

16. the champion cookie seller.
○

17. can you come to our
○

18. meeting on friday, may 2, and
○   ○   ○

19. tell us about it?
○

20. your friend, Jane
○   ○

Language Mechanics: Punctuation (CAT/CTBS)

Samples

A. I left my ball in the yard

○ .   ○ ,   ○ ?   ○ !   ○ none

B. Jill's new shoes are blue and white.

○ .   ○ ,   ○ ?   ○ !   ○ none

1. Did you like the magic show

○ .   ○ ,   ○ ?   ○ !   ○ none

2. Help

○ .   ○ ,   ○ ?   ○ !   ○ none

3. Put the box on the table

○ .   ○ ,   ○ ?   ○ !   ○ none

4. Will you come to my party

○ .   ○ ,   ○ ?   ○ !   ○ none

5. I went to my piano lesson

○ .   ○ ,   ○ ?   ○ !   ○ none

6. Why are you crying, Mary

○ .   ○ ,   ○ ?   ○ !   ○ none

7. Hooray

○ .   ○ ,   ○ ?   ○ !   ○ none

Language Mechanics: Punctuation (ITBS)

Samples

A.

○ My friend's cat had kittens
○ last week. I hope that I will get
○ to have one of them

B.

○ Stop The traffic is very
○ heavy here. Let's wait for a
○ new green light.

1.

○ Mr. Whitehead said to us,
○ The museum is over there.
○ We had finally arrived.

5.

○ It is too noisy in here,
○ said Tran. The movie theater
○ was having a kids' matinee.

2.

○ Next month we will have a
○ party for our parents. They
○ were married May 21 1985.

6.

○ We picked up all of our
○ toys and put them away. Mom
○ said it looked much neater

3.

○ My name is G L Cramer. I
○ like to be called by my initials.
○ It makes me feel special.

7.

○ Where are you going If you
○ are going to the store, may I go
○ with you?

4.

○ Has anyone seen my baseball
○ mitt I thought I left it on the
○ kitchen table.

8.

○ Help Please get the teacher.
○ Jill fell off a swing and
○ hurt herself.

Language Mechanics: Punctuation (ITBS)

Samples

Question Marks

A. Will Mr Johnson be your
○

B. troop leader next year
○   ○

Commas

C.   My uncle lives outside of
○

D. Jacksonville Florida
○   ○

Question Marks

1.   My little sister always asks
○

2. What is the moon made of
○

3. How far away is it
○

4. At times I feel like asking "Why
○   ○

5. don't you go there and see "
○

Commas

10.   I live at 123 Main Street in
○

11. Reno Nevada 89501. I was born
○   ○

12. on May 5 1987. My hobbies
○○   ○

13. are skating biking, and playing
○   ○

14. piano Now you know about me
○   ○

Periods

6.   Last week we went to a zoo
○   ○

7. Can you guess what we saw
○   ○

Apostrophes

15. Bills friend Jess doesnt like
○   ○   ○

16. math. So Bill helps Jess.
○   ○

Quotation Marks

8.   Randy said, Let's go to the
○   ○

9. mall. We can go shopping.
○   ○

Exclamation Points

17. When Katie received the medal
○   ○

18. she wanted to shout "Hooray "
○   ○

Language Mechanics: Punctuation (MAT/SAT/TAAS)

Samples

A.

The giraffe ate _____

- ○ leaves?
- ○ leaves!
- ○ leaves
- ○ leaves.

B.

Did you find your _____

- ○ book
- ○ book?
- ○ book.
- ○ book!

1.

Mary went to _____

- ○ practice
- ○ practice,
- ○ practice!
- ○ practice.

5.

Stop hurting _____

- ○ me
- ○ me?
- ○ me!
- ○ me.

2.

Aren't they going to _____

- ○ come!
- ○ come,
- ○ come.
- ○ come?

6.

Who can do the _____

- ○ problem
- ○ problem?
- ○ problem!
- ○ problem.

3.

Can you play this _____

- ○ afternoon.
- ○ afternoon?
- ○ afternoon!
- ○ afternoon,

7.

Where are you _____

- ○ going.
- ○ going
- ○ going?
- ○ going,

4.

His birthday is _____

- ○ tomorrow.
- ○ tomorrow?
- ○ tomorrow
- ○ tomorrow,

8.

The book is on the _____

- ○ table
- ○ table,
- ○ table.
- ○ table?

Language Mechanics: Capitalization and Punctuation
(Identifying Correct Sentences)

Samples

A.

○ Where's Mr. robbins?
○ The Book is on the table.
○ she will take care of my sister.
○ I went to the movies yesterday.

B.

○ He lives in New York City.
○ I live in Oakland California.
○ where is your mother today?
○ Thanksgiving is in november.

1.

○ On tuesday we get our uniforms.
○ His kitten's name is fluffy.
○ This book was written by ms. Black.
○ Please tell me when it's four o'clock.

4.

○ My shirt has a rip in it
○ did you remember your homework?
○ Maries letter was interesting.
○ He plays video games every day.

2.

○ The fourth of july is my favorite day.
○ Did you ever see a scary movie.
○ David knows a lot about computers.
○ that clown has a sad painted face.

5.

○ I wrote a letter to Polly,
○ I received your card today?
○ She lost her watch.
○ He has two dog's.

3.

○ We will graduate on June 10 2004.
○ What do you know about fractions?
○ Bill and i flew home from Canada.
○ Her baby sister had Pneumonia.

6.

○ He lives in Houston Texas.
○ He lives in Houston, texas.
○ He lives in houston, Texas.
○ He lives in Houston, Texas.

Language Mechanics: Capitalization and Punctuation
(Proofing for Errors)

Sample

Dear Alyce,

Last weekend we went to <u>Aspen colorado</u>.
                                    A.

My dad taught my brother and me how to ski.

A. ○ Aspen, colorado

○ aspen Colorado

○ Aspen, Colorado

○ correct as it is

<u>dear Uncle Fred</u>
          1.

How did you know that I like <u>skating Thank</u> you
                                              2.

for the video, <u>*The Winter Olympics*</u>. I love it.
                          3.

<u>love</u>
  4.

Betsy

1. ○ Dear Uncle Fred

○ Dear Uncle Fred,

○ dear Uncle Fred,

○ correct as it is

3. ○ The Winter olympics

○ The winter Olympics

○ The Winter Olympics

○ correct as it is

2. ○ skating. Thank

○ skating, thank

○ skating? Thank

○ correct as it is

4. ○ Love,

○ love,

○ Love.

○ correct as it is

Language Expression: Usage (Sentences)

Samples

A. Our friends_____a new car.
- ○ has
- ○ have

B. That airplane is flying too_____.
- ○ low   ○ lowly
- ○ lower   ○ lowest

1. We _____ a picture for each student.
- ○ is hanging
- ○ are hanging

2. Joe _____ television every evening.
- ○ watch
- ○ watches

3. The farmer has six _____ .
- ○ sheep
- ○ sheeps

4. I _____ a song after you do.
- ○ sang   ○ sings
- ○ will sing ○ has sung

5. Where are _____ new gloves?
- ○ Jenny   ○ Jenny's
- ○ Jennys' ○ Jennys

6. Study the answers _____ .
- ○ careful   ○ most careful
- ○ carefully ○ more careful

7. _____are going to the party.
- ○ Me and Jim ○ I and Jim
- ○ Jim and me ○ Jim and I

8. That _____ tire has a nail in it.
- ○ cars   ○ cars'
- ○ car's   ○ cars's

9. Those girls already lost _____ tickets.
- ○ there   ○ their
- ○ they're ○ them

10. I started a very _____ book.
- ○ long   ○ longest
- ○ longer ○ longly

11. Fran and José _____ research.
- ○ are doing
- ○ is doing

12. Some of the _____ are broken.
- ○ drinking fountains
- ○ drinking fountain

13. I _____ them last night.
- ○ see   ○ saw
- ○ seen   ○ will see

14. The bus _____ right now.
- ○ is coming
- ○ are coming

15. Give the package to _____ .
- ○ Jack and me
- ○ Jack and I

16. Your story is _____ than mine.
- ○ longer   ○ long
- ○ longest ○ longly

Language Expression: Usage (Passages)

Sample Directions: Read the story. Decide which word or group of words fits best in each blank.

Mary Elizabeth Monroe wanted to find the perfect present for her father's birthday. She __(A)__ out by getting dressed in her very best clothes. Then she asked her mother to drive her to the mall. They went to a photography studio where Mary Elizabeth had her picture taken.

When Mary Elizabeth gave the photograph to her father, everyone __(B)__ it was the perfect present.

A. ○ starting
   ○ had starting
   ○ started
   ○ starts

B. ○ thinked
   ○ thought
   ○ thinking
   ○ will think

I hope I can __(1)__ to Europe someday. I would like to see the Eiffel Tower in Paris and the Colosseum in Rome. But most of all, I would like to see the countryside. I want to go to the Alps in Switzerland and the Lake Country in England. If I could __(2)__ a vacation in Europe, I would write a book about it.

1. ○ going
   ○ gone
   ○ go
   ○ went

2. ○ spent
   ○ spending
   ○ spend
   ○ had spent

Last night we __(3)__ to an exciting event called "Nighttime at the Wild Animal Park." Many animals like to feed at night. Tall giraffes __(4)__ nibbling on leaves near the high platform where we stood to watch. Some bears __(5)__ to see what was going on. One of them was in such a hurry, he __(6)__ another bear down.

3. ○ go
   ○ goed
   ○ went
   ○ going

5. ○ coming
   ○ came
   ○ come
   ○ has come

4. ○ were
   ○ was
   ○ is
   ○ has been

6. ○ knock
   ○ knocks
   ○ knocked
   ○ knocking

Language Expression: Pronouns

Samples

A. Mary and Fred are at the park.

- ○ We
- ○ They
- ○ Us
- ○ You

B. Please put the ball in the box.

- ○ them
- ○ they
- ○ it
- ○ he

1. The children picked up the toys.

- ○ Him
- ○ They
- ○ She
- ○ He

5. Molly's toy is new.

- ○ Her
- ○ She
- ○ Our
- ○ Their

2. The two kittens slept in the sun.

- ○ We
- ○ They
- ○ It
- ○ She

6. Tom, Jeff, and I live nearby.

- ○ They
- ○ We
- ○ Us
- ○ Them

3. Let Pedro use the equipment now.

- ○ him
- ○ he
- ○ it
- ○ them

7. Jessica went to the beach yesterday.

- ○ Her
- ○ It
- ○ She
- ○ They

4. That toy belongs to Richard.

- ○ him
- ○ he
- ○ it
- ○ them

8. Please give the ball to Susan.

- ○ she
- ○ he
- ○ her
- ○ them

Language Expression: Sentences
(Subjects and Predicates: CAT/CTBS)

Samples

A. The clowns _____.

- ○ falling
- ○ are funny
- ○ having fun

B. _____ is full.

- ○ Almost always
- ○ Early or late
- ○ The school bus

1. My dad's car _____.

- ○ by the house
- ○ is getting old
- ○ big and blue

6. _____ feel frozen.

- ○ My ears
- ○ On the way
- ○ In the snow

2. _____ tastes very good.

- ○ Eat
- ○ We drink
- ○ Pizza

7. Tom and Phan _____.

- ○ on a trip
- ○ went to camp
- ○ spending the night

3. _____ dive into the pool.

- ○ The children
- ○ From the side
- ○ Off the board

8. The sky _____.

- ○ very blue
- ○ is getting dark
- ○ full of stars

4. The owl _____.

- ○ in the hole in the tree
- ○ flew away to its nest
- ○ high in the sky

9. _____ is full of cars.

- ○ The highway
- ○ Very crowded
- ○ Going home

5. _____ live on this block.

- ○ Many children
- ○ Near the school
- ○ A nearby park

10. Our school _____.

- ○ with the flag in front
- ○ is clean and new
- ○ a weekend carnival

Language Expression: Sentences
(Word Order: CAT/CTBS/MAT/TAAS)

Samples

A. Mother is coming now.

- ○ Mother coming is now?
- ○ Is Mother coming now?
- ○ Coming now Mother is?

B. Dad will cook the dinner.

- ○ Will Dad cook the dinner?
- ○ Dad will the dinner cook?
- ○ Cook the dinner will Dad?

1. The door is stuck.

- ○ Is stuck the door?
- ○ The door stuck is?
- ○ Is the door stuck?

6. John is sad.

- ○ Is John sad?
- ○ Sad is John?
- ○ John sad is?

2. I may go to the movies.

- ○ Go to the movies may I?
- ○ I to the movies may go?
- ○ May I go to the movies?

7. Betty can spell everything.

- ○ Everything can Betty spell?
- ○ Can Betty spell everything?
- ○ Betty everything can spell?

3. The train will stop.

- ○ Will the train stop?
- ○ Stop the train will?
- ○ Will stop the train?

8. Your riddles are funny.

- ○ Your funny are riddles?
- ○ Funny your riddles are?
- ○ Are your riddles funny?

4. Lupe can dance.

- ○ Dance Lupe can?
- ○ Can Lupe dance?
- ○ Lupe dance can?

9. She is my grandmother.

- ○ She my grandmother is?
- ○ My grandmother she is?
- ○ Is she my grandmother?

5. He will throw out the trash.

- ○ Will he throw out the trash?
- ○ The trash will he throw out?
- ○ Throw out will he the trash?

10. This is a good book.

- ○ A good book is this?
- ○ Is this a good book?
- ○ This a good book is?

Language Expression: Sentences
(Kind of Sentence: MAT/TAAS)

Sample

They ran fast

○	○	○
Telling	Asking	No Sentence

1.

Martin wants some milk

○	○	○
Telling	Asking	No Sentence

2.

Have you ever visited the zoo

○	○	○
Telling	Asking	No Sentence

3.

Going to the grocery store

○	○	○
Telling	Asking	No Sentence

4.

Does he plan to watch the game

○	○	○
Telling	Asking	No Sentence

5.

To the park by my house

○	○	○
Telling	Asking	No Sentence

6.

I returned the book yesterday

○	○	○
Telling	Asking	No Sentence

Language Expression: Sentences
(Complete Sentences: SAT)

Samples

A.

- ○ With a blue balloon.
- ○ José waited for his turn.
- ○ Passed him the ball.

B.

- ○ The store by the park.
- ○ Through wind and rain.
- ○ Maria plays the piano.

1.

- ○ Those are rain clouds.
- ○ Pink clouds in the west.
- ○ Looking out the window.

6.

- ○ With two overdue books.
- ○ Maria goes to the library.
- ○ Reading a good book.

2.

- ○ The dog loves her puppies.
- ○ Eating the dog food.
- ○ Spotted white and black.

7.

- ○ Holding my report card.
- ○ With excellent grades.
- ○ Mother will be happy.

3.

- ○ Ten candles on the cake.
- ○ Pink frosting and roses.
- ○ Today is my birthday.

8.

- ○ Under the garden gate.
- ○ My dog, Arfie, ran away.
- ○ Before it gets really dark.

4.

- ○ We walked home from school.
- ○ Carrying lots of paintings.
- ○ Many good television shows.

9.

- ○ Jumped rope really fast.
- ○ Lots of hard homework.
- ○ Where is your lunchbox?

5.

- ○ Two chocolate chip cookies.
- ○ I'm hungry for my lunch.
- ○ Standing in a long line.

10.

- ○ Always makes pancakes.
- ○ My brother feels happy.
- ○ Upstairs in my bedroom.

Language Expression: Sentences
(Proofing Passages: TAAS)

Sample Directions: Read the story. Decide which is the best way to write the underlined part. If it is correct, mark "no mistake."

One day a large sea turtle swam in from the ocean and climbed out on the beach. She dug a hole in the sand and laid many, many eggs. Then she went away. The sun warmed the eggs. <u>Finally, the tiny sea turtles. Crawled out on the sand.</u>

A.
○ Finally, tiny sea turtles out on the sand.
○ Finally, the tiny sea turtles crawled out on the sand.
○ The turtles who crawled out on the sand were sea creatures.
○ no mistake

<u>The rain was pouring down. When the football game began.</u> After
(1)
awhile the sun came out and dried the field. <u>By the end of the game,</u>
                                                    (2)
<u>everyone in the stadium was feeling too warm.</u>

1.
○ It was raining. And the football game began.
○ It was pouring. The game began in the rain.
○ The rain was pouring down when the football game began.
○ no mistake

2.
○ By the end of the game, everyone.
○ At the end of the game, everyone was warm.
○ By the end of the game, everyone in the stadium had warmed up.
○ no mistake

<u>The boxes were on a high shelf in the closet.</u> Kent and Clara had
(3)
nothing to stand on. <u>They were sure to knock everything down. if</u>
                              (4)
<u>they climbed on the shelves.</u>

3.
○ The boxes were. On a high shelf in the closet.
○ The boxes on a high shelf in the closet.
○ On a high shelf in the closet the boxes were.
○ no mistake

4.
○ They were sure. To knock everything down if they climbed on the shelves.
○ They were sure to knock everything down if they climbed on the shelves.
○ The shelves were sure to break. If they climbed on them.
○ no mistake

Language Expression: Sentence Sequence

Samples

A. (1) Mary and Sue went to practice.
(2) Finally, they played a game.
(3) Next, they did exercises.
- ○ 1 – 2 – 3
- ○ 1 – 3 – 2
- ○ 3 – 2 – 1

B. (1) They gathered their blocks.
(2) Then they built a castle.
(3) Meg and Dan wanted to build something.
- ○ 1 – 3 – 2
- ○ 2 – 3 – 1
- ○ 3 – 1 – 2

1. (1) Then she planted some flowers.
(2) Mother pulled all of the weeds.
(3) Later, Mother sat in her garden.
- ○ 1 – 2 – 3
- ○ 2 – 1 – 3
- ○ 3 – 2 – 1

2. (1) The team ran out on the field.
(2) They played a very good game.
(3) Then the coach bought ice cream.
- ○ 1 – 2 – 3
- ○ 2 – 1 – 3
- ○ 3 – 2 – 1

3. (1) The caterpillar ate and ate.
(2) It turned into a butterfly.
(3) It spun a cocoon around itself.
- ○ 1 – 3 – 2
- ○ 2 – 1 – 3
- ○ 3 – 2 – 1

4. (1) Fred had three kittens.
(2) Now Fred has one kitten.
(3) He gave two kittens away.
- ○ 1 – 3 – 2
- ○ 2 – 3 – 1
- ○ 3 – 2 – 1

5. (1) First we learned to add.
(2) Our class studied math.
(3) Then we learned to subtract.
- ○ 1 – 3 – 2
- ○ 2 – 3 – 1
- ○ 2 – 1 – 3

6. (1) We loaded suitcases in the car.
(2) First, we packed our clothes.
(3) Then we left for our vacation.
- ○ 1 – 3 – 2
- ○ 2 – 3 – 1
- ○ 2 – 1 – 3

Language Expression: Paragraphs

Sample

Javier was going to join a scouting troop._____. He would also get to go camping.

- ○ Scouting is very fun.
- ○ He would make new friends.
- ○ Javier has two pet cats.
- ○ Javier enjoys many sports.

1. The bird gathered bits of string and small sticks. _____. Soon she would lay her eggs.

- ○ The wind blew the tree.
- ○ She made them into a nest.
- ○ The bird had a yellow bill.
- ○ I think it is a blue jay.

2. My father's birthday is next week._____. He will enjoy blowing out the candles.

- ○ He made a great kite for me.
- ○ He is six feet tall.
- ○ We will buy some presents.
- ○ I am going to make a cake.

3. Mary decided to clean her room._____. Then she sat down to rest.

- ○ First she picked up all of her toys.
- ○ Then she went out to play.
- ○ She missed her best friend.
- ○ Mary's room was very messy.

4. The school bus was late this morning._____. My friend will help me catch up.

- ○ I missed math class.
- ○ We all waited on the corner.
- ○ Freddy decided to walk.
- ○ The bus is yellow and black.

5. Our class is going on a field trip._____. We will see many dinosaur bones.

- ○ We are going to the beach.
- ○ We all brought sack lunches.
- ○ We will be gone all day.
- ○ We are going to a museum.

6. Jerry and Buzz went to the beach._____. A big wave washed it away.

- ○ They found many seashells.
- ○ They built a huge sandcastle.
- ○ The ocean was blue and green.
- ○ Do you like to swim in the waves?

Language Expression: Descriptive Writing (TAAS)

This picture is about some children having fun at a circus. Look at the picture and write a story about what you see.

Language Expression: Informative Writing (TAAS)

Suppose you are planning to fix dinner for your family. Write a story about what you will have to do. Tell about what you must do first. Then tell about all of the other things you must do.

Language Expression: Narrative Writing (TAAS)

Imagine that you have found a magic ring that will grant you three wishes. Write a story about what you would wish for and what would happen when you got your wishes.

Work-Study Skills: Maps (ITBS)

Samples

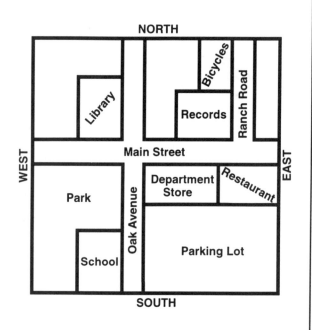

A. You are walking west on Main Street. What is on your left after you cross Oak Avenue?

○ the library

○ the department store

○ the park

B. From which street could you enter the parking lot?

○ Oak Avenue

○ Main Street

○ Ranch Road

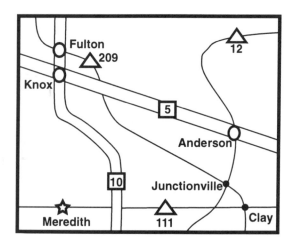

1. Which roads cross in Junctionville?

○ 12 and 209

○ 10 and 5

○ 12 and 111

2. Which city is the state capital?

○ Fulton

○ Meredith

○ Anderson

3. In which direction should you go to get from Meredith to Clay?

○ east

○ west

○ north

Work-Study Skills: Graphs/Tables (ITBS)

Samples

SCIENCE CENTER—TASKS COMPLETED	
Gina	★ ★ ★ ★
Tom	★ ★ ★ ★ ★
Mario	★ ★ ★
Tran	★
Rick	★ ★ ★ ★

A. How many tasks did Mario complete?
- ○ 3
- ○ 4
- ○ 5

B. Who completed the same number of tasks as Gina?
- ○ Tom
- ○ Mario
- ○ Rick

PLAYGROUND EQUIPMENT	School	Park
Slides	2	3
Swings	4	6
Bars	2	2
Merry-Go-Rounds	1	2
Tunnels	0	3

3. Of which equipment does the park have the most?
- ○ slides
- ○ swings
- ○ tunnels

4. At the school, how many more swings are there than slides?
- ○ 2
- ○ 3
- ○ 4

1. How many slides are there at the school and the park in all?
- ○ 2   ○ 3   ○ 5

2. How many merry-go-rounds are at the park?
- ○ 1   ○ 2   ○ 3

5. There is the same number of which type of equipment at the school and the park?
- ○ slides
- ○ bars
- ○ tunnels

Work-Study Skills: Alphabetizing (ITBS/SAT/MAT)

Samples

A. ○ penny

○ dog

○ king

B. ○ bring

○ brought

○ brown

1. ○ friend

○ funny

○ fort

6. ○ stop

○ go

○ wait

2. ○ stand

○ star

○ step

7. ○ train

○ window

○ yellow

3. ○ hand

○ many

○ jam

8. ○ rain

○ ran

○ rattle

4. ○ throw

○ three

○ thrill

9. ○ wind

○ little

○ tree

5. ○ present

○ cake

○ birthday

10. ○ computer

○ calculator

○ printer

Work-Study Skills: Alphabetical Order (ITBS)

Samples

A. Which picture should be at the very top of the page?

    rabbit   apple   dog
     ◯   ◯   ◯

B. Which picture should be between the rabbit and the zebra?

    hoe   dog   watch
    ◯   ◯   ◯

1. Which picture should be the second one on the page?

    balloon   dog   rabbit
     ◯   ◯   ◯

4. Which picture should be between the apple and the dog?

    balloon   hoe   watch
     ◯   ◯   ◯

2. Which picture should be right after the watch?

    rabbit   zebra   apple
     ◯   ◯   ◯

5. Which picture should be right after the dog?

    watch   hoe   rabbit
     ◯   ◯   ◯

3. Which picture should be right before the hoe?

    balloon   apple   dog
     ◯   ◯   ◯

6. Which picture should be the last one on the page?

    zebra   watch   apple
     ◯   ◯   ◯

Student Practice Page

Work-Study Skills: Table of Contents

Sample

In the Mountains Table of Contents		
Chapter		Page
1	Winter Sports	1
2	Hiking	10
3	Climbing	20
4	Nature Trails	25

A. On which pages will you learn about skiing?

- ○ 1–9
- ○ 10–19
- ○ 20–24

Alaska Table of Contents		
Chapter		Page
1	Geography of Alaska	1
2	The Largest State	20
3	Tourist Attractions	35
4	Life of the People	41

1. Which pages would tell you when Alaska became a state?

- ○ 1–19
- ○ 20–34
- ○ 35–40

2. Which pages would tell you about Alaska's mountain ranges?

- ○ 1–19
- ○ 20–34
- ○ 35–40

3. On which page should you start reading to learn about the dog-sled races held every year during March?

- ○ 20
- ○ 35
- ○ 41

4. On which page should you start reading to learn about the schools in Alaska?

- ○ 20
- ○ 35
- ○ 41

120

Work-Study Skills: Classifying (ITBS)

Samples

A.   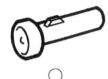
     ○   ○   ○   ○

B.   yawn   cry   happy   laugh
     ○   ○   ○   ○

1.   
     ○   ○   ○   ○

2.   minute   time   second   hour
     ○   ○   ○   ○

3.   his   my   our   them
     ○   ○   ○   ○

4.   library   hospital   school   door
     ○   ○   ○   ○

5.   hot   touch   cold   warm
     ○   ○   ○   ○

6.   lettuce   carrot   potato   banana
     ○   ○   ○   ○

7.   
     ○   ○   ○   ○

Work-Study Skills: Reference Materials (ITBS)

Samples

A. To find out how to get to a local museum, where should you look?

○ at a clock
○ on a globe
○ on a street map

B. Which can you use to learn about elephants?

○ a book about pets
○ a book about wild animals
○ a storybook

1. One place to look for the time a television show starts is . . .

○ a calendar.
○ a newspaper.
○ an atlas.

4. Where could you find out how many days are in the month of September?

○ on a clock
○ on a calendar
○ on a birthday card

2. Where should you look to find the name of the person who wrote a book you are reading?

○ in the index
○ in the table of contents
○ on the title page

5. Which word should you look up in a dictionary to find out if broccoli is a fruit or a vegetable?

○ broccoli
○ fruit
○ vegetable

3. Where should you look to find the capital city of Canada?

○ in a telephone book
○ in an atlas
○ in a newspaper

6. You want to bake a carrot cake. In which book should you look?

○ *Planting a Garden*
○ *Kids Can Cook*
○ *How to Make Soup*

Math: Computation—Addition (No Regrouping)

Samples

A.

$$\begin{array}{r} 5 \\ + \ 3 \\ \hline \end{array}$$

53 ○
8 ○
9 ○
2 ○

B.

$1 + 6 + 2 =$

7 ○
10 ○
12 ○
9 ○

1.

$$\begin{array}{r} 41 \\ + \ 12 \\ \hline \end{array}$$

18 ○
8 ○
15 ○
53 ○

6.

$6 + 3 + 0 =$

9 ○
8 ○
6 ○
63 ○

2.

$3 + 3 + 2 =$

9 ○
18 ○
80 ○
8 ○

7.

$$\begin{array}{r} 42 \\ + \ \ 3 \\ \hline \end{array}$$

45 ○
52 ○
40 ○
67 ○

3.

$$\begin{array}{r} 42 \\ + \ 22 \\ \hline \end{array}$$

22 ○
60 ○
64 ○
20 ○

8.

$$\begin{array}{r} 35 \\ + \ \ 2 \\ \hline \end{array}$$

77 ○
17 ○
37 ○
73 ○

4.

$$\begin{array}{r} 3 \\ 4 \\ + \ 2 \\ \hline \end{array}$$

9 ○
12 ○
11 ○
7 ○

9.

$$\begin{array}{r} 53 \\ + \ 45 \\ \hline \end{array}$$

8 ○
98 ○
18 ○
89 ○

5.

$$\begin{array}{r} 56 \\ + \ \ 3 \\ \hline \end{array}$$

86 ○
88 ○
53 ○
59 ○

10.

$$\begin{array}{r} 40 \\ + \ 10 \\ \hline \end{array}$$

30 ○
40 ○
50 ○
10 ○

Math: Computation—Addition (Regrouping)

Samples

A.
$$\begin{array}{r} 6 \\ + 5 \\ \hline \end{array}$$

- ○ 13
- ○ 11
- ○ 1
- ○ 12

B.
$$42 + 28 =$$

- ○ 16
- ○ 60
- ○ 70
- ○ 72

1.
$$\begin{array}{r} 7 \\ + 4 \\ \hline \end{array}$$

- ○ 1
- ○ 10
- ○ 11
- ○ 9

6.
$$\begin{array}{r} 123 \\ + 797 \\ \hline \end{array}$$

- ○ 820
- ○ 810
- ○ 910
- ○ 920

2.
$$\begin{array}{r} 15 \\ + 26 \\ \hline \end{array}$$

- ○ 31
- ○ 38
- ○ 41
- ○ 48

7.
$$\begin{array}{r} 5 \\ 7 \\ + 3 \\ \hline \end{array}$$

- ○ 10
- ○ 12
- ○ 15
- ○ 16

3.
$$7 + 6 =$$

- ○ 1
- ○ 13
- ○ 42
- ○ 76

8.
$$\begin{array}{r} 2096 \\ + 5932 \\ \hline \end{array}$$

- ○ 8968
- ○ 8978
- ○ 8028
- ○ 8868

4.
$$\begin{array}{r} 87 \\ + 45 \\ \hline \end{array}$$

- ○ 132
- ○ 122
- ○ 120
- ○ 142

9.
$$\begin{array}{r} 90 \\ + 60 \\ \hline \end{array}$$

- ○ 30
- ○ 96
- ○ 130
- ○ 150

5.
$$\begin{array}{r} 47 \\ 35 \\ + \ 5 \\ \hline \end{array}$$

- ○ 77
- ○ 83
- ○ 87
- ○ 97

10.
$$\begin{array}{r} 9 \\ + 5 \\ \hline \end{array}$$

- ○ 4
- ○ 14
- ○ 59
- ○ 95

Math: Computation—Subtraction (No Regrouping)

Samples

A.

$$\begin{array}{r} 6 \\ - 4 \\ \hline \end{array}$$

- 10 ○
- 6 ○
- 4 ○
- 2 ○

B.

$$\begin{array}{r} 77 \\ - \ 6 \\ \hline \end{array}$$

- 17 ○
- 11 ○
- 71 ○
- 61 ○

1.

$$\begin{array}{r} 8 \\ - 2 \\ \hline \end{array}$$

- 6 ○
- 8 ○
- 10 ○
- 2 ○

6.

$$\begin{array}{r} 58 \\ - 15 \\ \hline \end{array}$$

- 33 ○
- 43 ○
- 63 ○
- 73 ○

2.

$$\begin{array}{r} 12 \\ - 8 \\ \hline \end{array}$$

- 20 ○
- 16 ○
- 4 ○
- 8 ○

7.

$$\begin{array}{r} 60 \\ - 10 \\ \hline \end{array}$$

- 70 ○
- 60 ○
- 50 ○
- 10 ○

3.

$$\begin{array}{r} 45 \\ - \ 4 \\ \hline \end{array}$$

- 49 ○
- 10 ○
- 41 ○
- 44 ○

8.

$$\begin{array}{r} 56 \\ - \ 3 \\ \hline \end{array}$$

- 49 ○
- 43 ○
- 53 ○
- 59 ○

4.

$$\begin{array}{r} 55 \\ - 11 \\ \hline \end{array}$$

- 11 ○
- 66 ○
- 44 ○
- 55 ○

9.

$9 - 9 =$

- 18 ○
- 10 ○
- 9 ○
- 0 ○

5.

$12 - 6 =$

- 5 ○
- 6 ○
- 10 ○
- 18 ○

10.

$$\begin{array}{r} 38 \\ - \ 5 \\ \hline \end{array}$$

- 43 ○
- 33 ○
- 23 ○
- 15 ○

Math: Computation—Subtraction (Regrouping)

Samples

A.

$$82 - 56$$

- ○ 136
- ○ 36
- ○ 26
- ○ 32

B.

$$63 - 8 =$$

- ○ 71
- ○ 75
- ○ 55
- ○ 65

1.

$$8 - 6$$

- ○ 14
- ○ 12
- ○ 4
- ○ 2

6.

$$252 - 136$$

- ○ 116
- ○ 126
- ○ 388
- ○ 398

2.

$$14 - 8 =$$

- ○ 22
- ○ 14
- ○ 8
- ○ 6

7.

$$764 - 569$$

- ○ 195
- ○ 115
- ○ 205
- ○ 215

3.

$$52 - 47$$

- ○ 5
- ○ 15
- ○ 89
- ○ 99

8.

$$719 - 428$$

- ○ 311
- ○ 301
- ○ 291
- ○ 201

4.

$$75 - 6$$

- ○ 79
- ○ 69
- ○ 71
- ○ 61

9.

$$50 - 5 =$$

- ○ 250
- ○ 55
- ○ 45
- ○ 35

5.

$$809 - 215$$

- ○ 514
- ○ 504
- ○ 594
- ○ 694

10.

$$26 - 7$$

- ○ 19
- ○ 21
- ○ 23
- ○ 29

Math: Computation—Multiplication (with Pictures)

Directions: Do each multiplication problem. Fill in the circle for the answer that you think is correct.

Sample

Mr. Wilson gave 2 candy bars each to Franklin, Pham, and José. How many candy bars did he give them in all? Fill in the circle next to your answer.

○ 2
○ 3
○ 6
○ 12

Franklin   Pham   José

1. Ms. Anderson, the school secretary, sharpened some new pencils. She put 4 pencils into each of 3 containers. She put one container on the principal's desk, one on the school nurse's desk, and one on her own desk. Which picture shows the right number of pencils and containers? Fill in the circle next to your answer.

2. It takes 4 cups of punch to fill a pitcher. Betsy wants to fill 3 pitchers with punch. How many cups of punch will she need? Fill in the circle next to your answer.

○ 4 cups ○ 8 cups
○ 10 cups ○ 12 cups

3. Lupe and Kelly each decorated 6 eggs. They want to display them together. Which container will hold all of their eggs? Fill in the circle next to your answer.

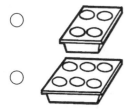 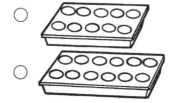

Math: Computation—Multiplication

Samples

A.

$4 \times 7 =$

- ○ 11
- ○ 74
- ○ 28
- ○ 21
- ○ none of these

B.

```
  31
x  2
----
```

- ○ 72
- ○ 63
- ○ 61
- ○ 32
- ○ none of these

1.

```
   7
x  8
----
```

- ○ 56
- ○ 64
- ○ 76
- ○ 81
- ○ none of these

6.

```
  43
x  9
----
```

- ○ 52
- ○ 367
- ○ 387
- ○ 3627
- ○ none of these

2.

```
  28
x  0
----
```

- ○ 0
- ○ 28
- ○ 280
- ○ 2800
- ○ none of these

7.

$6 \times 8 =$

- ○ 14
- ○ 40
- ○ 42
- ○ 46
- ○ none of these

3.

```
   9
x  1
----
```

- ○ 1
- ○ 9
- ○ 10
- ○ 19
- ○ none of these

8.

```
   3
x  0
----
```

- ○ 0
- ○ 3
- ○ 30
- ○ 33
- ○ none of these

4.

```
  871
x   5
-----
```

- ○ 876
- ○ 4055
- ○ 4355
- ○ 8715
- ○ none of these

9.

```
  25
x  4
----
```

- ○ 29
- ○ 80
- ○ 100
- ○ 254
- ○ none of these

5.

```
   5
x  5
----
```

- ○ 5
- ○ 10
- ○ 15
- ○ 20
- ○ none of these

10.

```
  400
x   3
-----
```

- ○ 12
- ○ 120
- ○ 403
- ○ 1200
- ○ none of these

Math: Computation—Division (with Pictures)

Directions: Do the sample below with your teacher. Then complete each division problem. Fill in the circle for the answer that you think is correct.

Sample

There are 6 ice cream bars in a package. A group of 3 friends wanted to share the package so that they each would get the same number of ice cream bars. How many ice cream bars would each friend get? Fill in the circle next to your answer.

○ 2
○ 3
○ 5
○ 9

1. Mario was staying in a cabin in the forest. He had 12 bottles of water. He knew he would use 2 bottles of water a day. How many days could Mario plan to stay? Fill in the circle next to your answer.

○ 2   ○ 6
○ 12   ○ 14

2. Millie mixed milk and pudding mix to make 16 ounces of pudding. Her serving dishes will each hold 4 ounces. If she fills each dish right to the top, how many dishes can she fill? Fill in the circle next to your answer.

3. Jason is putting science folders together. Each folder needs 3 brads. He has 15 3-inch brads. How many folders can he put together? Fill in the circle next to your answer.

○ 2   ○ 3
○ 5   ○ 15

Math: Computation—Division

Samples

A.

$4\overline{)84}$

- ○ 12
- ○ 20
- ○ 23
- ○ 31
- ○ none of these

B.

$9 \div 6 =$

- ○ 1
- ○ 1 R 3
- ○ 2
- ○ 2 R 1
- ○ none of these

1.

$6 \div 2 =$

- ○ 8
- ○ 12
- ○ 3
- ○ 41
- ○ none of these

6.

$6\overline{)8}$

- ○ 2
- ○ 2
- ○ 1 R 2
- ○ 2 R 1
- ○ none of these

2.

$2\overline{)40}$

- ○ 10
- ○ 20
- ○ 2
- ○ 15
- ○ none of these

7.

$48 \div 6 =$

- ○ 9
- ○ 8
- ○ 7
- ○ 6
- ○ none of these

3.

$3\overline{)69}$

- ○ 20
- ○ 23
- ○ 30
- ○ 32
- ○ none of these

8.

$9\overline{)9}$

- ○ 0
- ○ 1
- ○ 9
- ○ 81
- ○ none of these

4.

$4\overline{)10}$

- ○ 2
- ○ 2 R 2
- ○ 2 R 3
- ○ 3
- ○ none of these

9.

$4\overline{)44}$

- ○ 1
- ○ 10
- ○ 11
- ○ 40
- ○ none of these

5.

$2\overline{)68}$

- ○ 30
- ○ 33
- ○ 43
- ○ 60
- ○ none of these

10.

$11\overline{)110}$

- ○ 1
- ○ 10
- ○ 11
- ○ 100
- ○ none of these

Math: Concepts/Applications—Patterns/Sequence/Order

Sample

1.

2.

3.

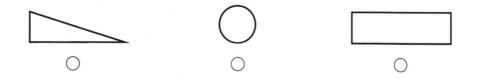

Math: Concepts/Applications—Numeration

Sample

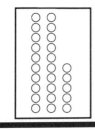

10	15	25	35
○	○	○	○

1.

$$7, \underline{\quad\quad}, 9$$

6	8	9	10
○	○	○	○

2.

95	509	59	950
○	○	○	○

3.

			tens ‖ ones
43	40 + 7	five tens	5 ‖ 4
○	○	○	○

4.

☐ **> 64**

13	45	71	59
○	○	○	○

5.

42	404	345	64
○	○	○	○

6.

○	○	○	○

Math: Concepts/Applications—Number Families

Sample

5 + 4 = 9	9 − 4 = 5
4 + 5 = 9	_____

5 − 4 = 1 ○   9 − 5 = 4 ○   9 + 5 = 14 ○   9 − 0 = 9 ○

1.

5 − 2 = 3 ○   2 + 3 = 5 ○   1 + 4 = 5 ○   5 − 3 = 2 ○

2.

4 + 3 = 7

7 − 3 = 4 ○   7 + 4 = 11 ○   7 + 3 = 10 ○   4 − 3 = 1 ○

3.

7 + 5 = 12	12 − 7 = 5
_____	12 − 5 = 7

12 + 7 = 19 ○   5 + 12 = 17 ○   7 − 5 = 2 ○   5 + 7 = 12 ○

4.

6 + 7 = 13 ○   13 − 7 = 6 ○   7 − 6 = 1 ○   7 + 6 = 13 ○

5.

8 + 7 = 15

8 − 7 = 1 ○   15 + 7 = 22 ○   15 − 8 = 7 ○   15 + 8 = 23 ○

6.

6 + 2 = 8	_____
2 + 6 = 8	8 − 6 = 2

6 − 2 = 4 ○   8 + 2 = 10 ○   8 + 6 = 14 ○   8 − 2 = 6 ○

Student Practice Page

Math: Concepts/Applications—Number Sentences/Theory (1)

Samples

A. Which number will make the number sentence true?

$$\boxed{} + 7 = 11$$

○ 3   ○ 4
○ 5   ○ 18

B. Which number will make the number sentence true?

$$2 + \boxed{} = 6$$

○ 4   ○ 5
○ 6   ○ 7

1. Which number will make the number sentence true?

$$352 + 15 = \boxed{} + 352$$

○ 15   ○ 352
○ 51   ○ 325

4. Which number will make the number sentence true?

$$25 + \boxed{} > 33 + 33$$

○ 25   ○ 35
○ 30   ○ 45

2. Which number will make both number sentences true?

$$18 - \boxed{} = 7$$
$$7 + \boxed{} = 18$$

○ 9   ○ 7
○ 11   ○ 18

5. Which number will make the number sentence true?

$$25 + \boxed{} < 22 + 22$$

○ 15   ○ 30
○ 20   ○ 35

3. $6 + n = 13$. So n equals . . .

○ 6   ○ 8
○ 7   ○ 9

6. $18 - n = 9$. So n equals . . .

○ 9   ○ 8
○ 7   ○ 10

Math: Concepts/Applications—Number Sentences/Theory (2)

Samples

A. Which sign will make the number sentence true?

$$8 + 10 = 9 \boxed{} 2$$

○ +   ○ x

○ −   ○ ÷

B. Which shows two even numbers?

○ 3, 10
○ 5, 9
○ 1, 8
○ 4, 14

1. Which number will make the number sentence true?

$$\boxed{} \times 4 = 24$$

○ 4   ○ 6

○ 5   ○ 8

4. Which shows two odd numbers?

○ 5, 10
○ 3, 11
○ 6, 9
○ 9, 12

2. Which number will make both number sentences true?

$$8 \times \boxed{} = 56$$
$$56 \div \boxed{} = 8$$

○ 6   ○ 7

○ 8   ○ 9

5. Which sign will make the number sentence true?

$$30 \div 5 \boxed{} 20 \div 2$$

○ <   ○ >

○ =   ○ x

3. $7 \times n = 21$. So **n** equals . . .

○ 2   ○ 4

○ 3   ○ 5

6. $18 \div n = 9$. So **n** equals . . .

○ 1   ○ 3

○ 2   ○ 4

Math: Concepts/Applications—Whole Numbers

Samples

A.

43	54	63	530
○	○	○	○

1.

- ○ 3 + 7 = 10
- ○ 7 + 10 = 17
- ○ 7 − 3 = 10
- ○ 3 + 4 = 7

2.
- ○ 15 − 6 = 19
- ○ 9 − 6 = 3
- ○ 9 + 6 = 15
- ○ 15 − 9 = 6

3.

560	506	5 + 6	56
○	○	○	○

4.

79 − 12 = ☐

60	70	75	90
○	○	○	○

5.

B.

400	420	425	450
○	○	○	○

6.
- ○ fifty-eight
- ○ five hundred eight
- | 580 | ○ fifty-eight hundred
- ○ five hundred eighty

7.

22	23	24	28
○	○	○	○

8.

11	12	35	75
○	○	○	○

9.

15	20	25	30
○	○	○	○

10.

three thousand fourteen

3,014	3,041	3,140	30,014
○	○	○	○

Math: Concepts/Applications—Place Value

Samples

A.	ones	tens	hundreds	thousands
86<u>2</u>	○	○	○	○
B.	94	49	409	904
	○	○	○	○

1.	ones	tens	hundreds	thousands
<u>7</u>1	○	○	○	○
2.	128	821	281	218
	○	○	○	○

3.	ones	tens	hundreds	thousands
23<u>5</u>	○	○	○	○
4.	365	563	635	356
	○	○	○	○
5.	723	237	273	327
	○	○	○	○
6.	1	5	6	2
1,562	○	○	○	○
7.	3	8	4	9
3,849	○	○	○	○
8.	1	0	2	5
1,025	○	○	○	○

Math: Concepts/Applications — Fractions

Samples

A

○   ○   ○   ○

B.

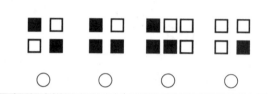
○   ○   ○   ○

1.

○   ○   ○   ○

6.

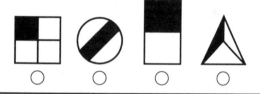
○   ○   ○   ○

2.

○   ○   ○   ○

7.

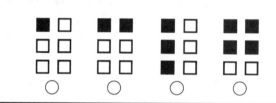
○   ○   ○   ○

3.

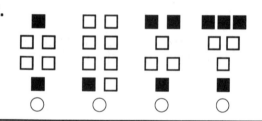
○   ○   ○   ○

8.

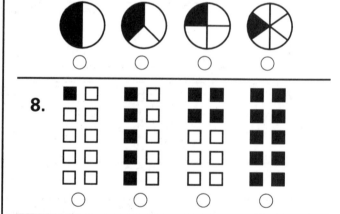
○   ○   ○   ○

4.

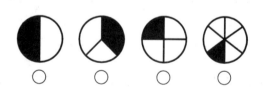
○   ○   ○   ○

9.

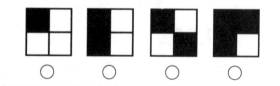
○   ○   ○   ○

5.

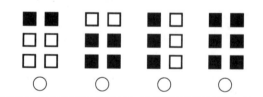
○   ○   ○   ○

10.

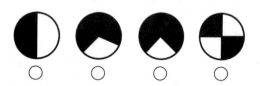
○   ○   ○   ○

Math: Concepts/Applications—Money (1)

Sample

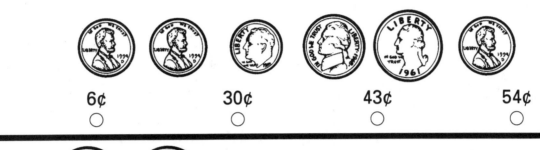

6¢	30¢	43¢	54¢
○	○	○	○

1.

45¢	54¢	81¢	90¢
○	○	○	○

2.

9¢	52¢	72¢	45¢
○	○	○	○

3.

9¢	53¢	57¢	93¢
○	○	○	○

4.

14¢	30¢	70¢	65¢
○	○	○	○

5.

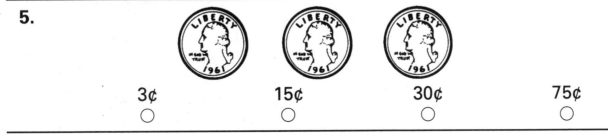

3¢	15¢	30¢	75¢
○	○	○	○

Math: Concepts/Applications—Money (2)

Sample

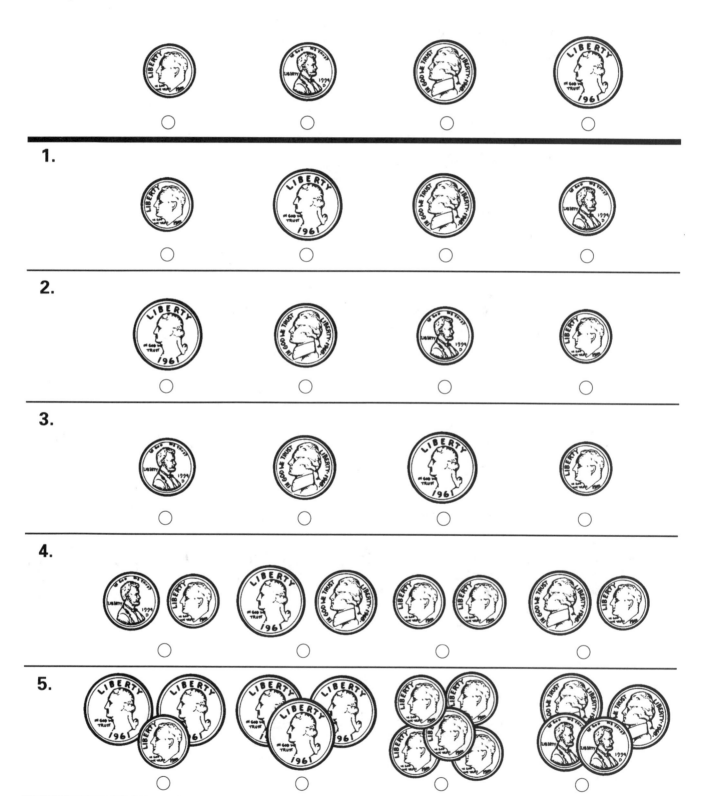

Math: Concepts/Applications—Graphs

Sample

Dry Days	
April	☼ ☼ ☼
May	☼ ☼ ☼ ☼ ☼
June	☼ ☼ ☼ ☼
July	☼ ☼ ☼ ☼
Aug.	☼ ☼ ☼
Sept.	☼ ☼
Each ☼ = 1 Dry Day	

A. In which month were there the fewest dry days?
- ○ April
- ○ May
- ○ August
- ○ September

B. How many more dry days were there in May than in August?
- ○ 1
- ○ 2
- ○ 3
- ○ 4

C. How many dry days were there in May and June altogether?
- ○ 4
- ○ 5
- ○ 8
- ○ 9

Books Read	
Randy	📖 📖 📖 📖
Jon	📖 📖 📖 📖 📖
Lili	📖 📖 📖
Kris	📖 📖
Sung	📖 📖 📖 📖 📖 📖
Pat	📖 📖 📖 📖
Each 📖 = 2 Books	

1. How many books did Lili read?
- ○ 3
- ○ 4
- ○ 5
- ○ 6

2. Which two students read the same number of books?
- ○ Randy and Pat
- ○ Jon and Sung
- ○ Lili and Kris
- ○ Randy and Lili

3. How many more books did Sung read than Kris?
- ○ 2
- ○ 4
- ○ 6
- ○ 8

4. How many books did the students read in all?
- ○ 24
- ○ 28
- ○ 40
- ○ 48

Math: Concepts/Applications—Geometry (1)

Samples

A

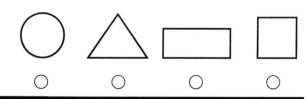

⚪ ⚪ ⚪ ⚪

B.

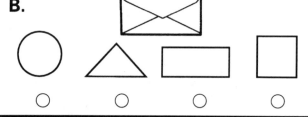

⚪ ⚪ ⚪ ⚪

1.

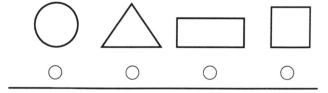

⚪ ⚪ ⚪ ⚪

6.

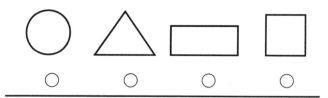

⚪ ⚪ ⚪ ⚪

2.

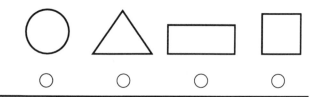

⚪ ⚪ ⚪ ⚪

7.

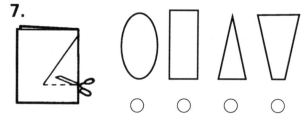

⚪ ⚪ ⚪ ⚪

3.

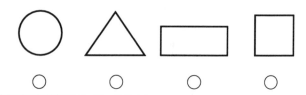

⚪ ⚪ ⚪ ⚪

8.

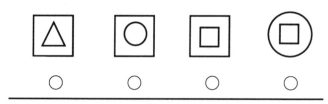

⚪ ⚪ ⚪ ⚪

4.

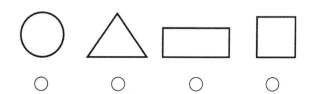

⚪ ⚪ ⚪ ⚪

9.

   1   2   3   4

⚪ ⚪ ⚪ ⚪

5.

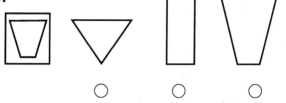

⚪ ⚪ ⚪

10.

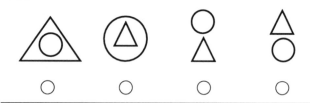

⚪ ⚪ ⚪ ⚪

Math: Concepts/Applications—Geometry (2)

Samples

A.
        ○   ○   ○   ○

B.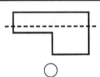
 ○   ○   ○   ○

1.   rectangle   circle   triangle   square
            ○   ○   ○   ○

2.
   ○   ○   ○   ○

3.
        ○   ○   ○   ○

4.   cylinder   sphere   cone   cube
           ○   ○   ○   ○

5.   cylinder   sphere   cone   cube
           ○   ○   ○   ○

6.
   ○   ○   ○   ○

7.
  ○   ○   ○   ○

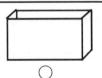

Math: Concepts/Applications—Measurement (1)

Sample

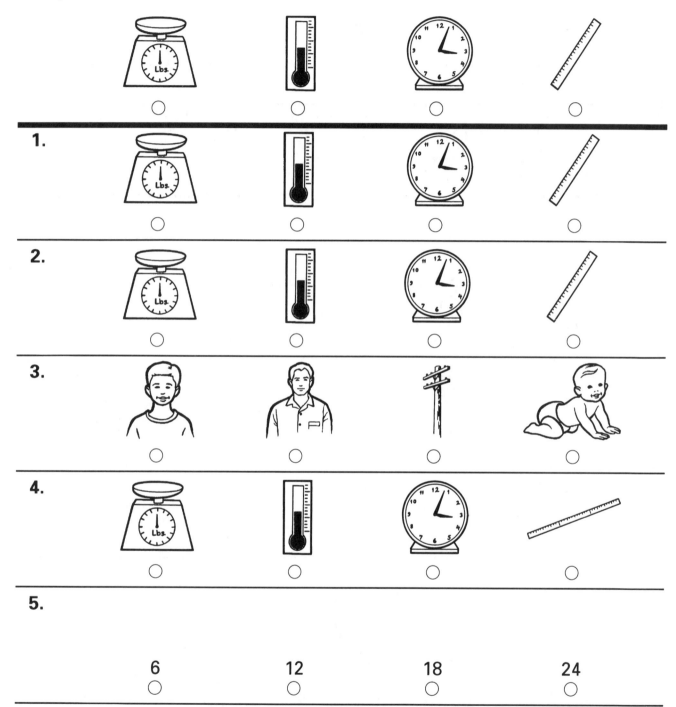

5.

| 6 | 12 | 18 | 24 |
| ○ | ○ | ○ | ○ |

6.

| 1 | 2 | 3 | 4 |
| ○ | ○ | ○ | ○ |

Math: Concepts/Applications—Measurement (2)

Samples

A.   ○ 3:08   ○ 8:03

○ 3:40   ○ 8:20

B.   ○ 12:30   ○ 1:30

○ 6:05   ○ 12:50

1.   ○ 10:12   ○ 12:10

○ 10:00   ○ 12:50

2.  2:45    ○   ○   ○   ○

3.  ○ 1:30   ○ 1:06

○ 6:05   ○ 6:01

4.    ○ 9:03   ○ 3:45

○ 9:15   ○ 3:09

5.   ○ 6:07   ○ 6:30

○ 7:06   ○ 7:30

6.  10:20   ○    ○   ○    ○

Math: Concepts/Applications—Measurement (3)

March						
Sun.	Mon.	Tues.	Wed.	Thurs.	Fri.	Sat.
	1	2	3	4	5	6
7	8	9	10	11	12	13
14	15	16	17	18	19	20
21	22	23	24	25	26	27
28	29	30	31			

1. On which day of the week does this month begin?

   Sunday ○ Monday ○ Friday ○ Tuesday ○

2. On which day of the week does March 17 fall?

   Sunday ○ Wednesday ○ Thursday ○ Saturday ○

3. The fourth Friday of this month falls on which date?

   19 ○ 20 ○ 25 ○ 26 ○

4. How many days does March have?

   28 ○ 29 ○ 30 ○ 31 ○

Math: Concepts/Applications — Measurement (4)

1. What temperature is shown on this thermometer?

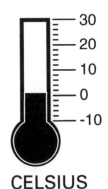

CELSIUS

○ 0° C   ○ 2° C

○ 1° C   ○ 5° C

2. How much does the rock weigh?

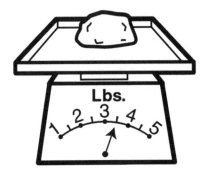

○ 31 lbs.   ○ 3 ½ lbs.

○ 41 lbs.   ○ 5 lbs.

3. How long is this pencil?

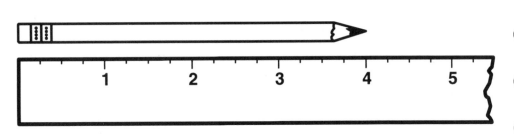

○ 2 inches

○ 3 inches

○ 4 inches

○ 5 inches

4. How long is the stick?

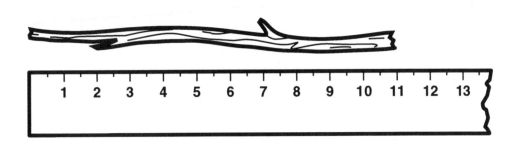

○ 9 cm

○ 10 cm

○ 11 cm

○ 12 cm

Math: Concepts/Applications — Problem Solving
(Adding with Pictures)

Sample

1.

      6 − 3 = 3   3 + 3 = 6   6 + 0 = 6   6 − 0 = 6
   ○   ○   ○   ○

2. 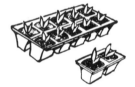   10   11   12   13
   ○   ○   ○   ○

3.    2   4   6   10
   ○   ○   ○   ○

4.    1   2   3   5
   ○   ○   ○   ○

5.   5   3   2   1
   ○   ○   ○   ○

6.    1   2   3   4
   ○   ○   ○   ○

Math: Concepts/Applications—Problem Solving
(Subtracting with Pictures)

Sample

2	3	1	5
○	○	○	○

1.

2	1	5	3
○	○	○	○

2.
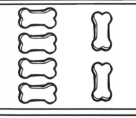

0	2	4	6
○	○	○	○

3.
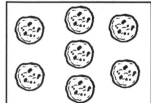

7	4	3	1
○	○	○	○

4.

1	2	4	6
○	○	○	○

5.

4	3	2	1
○	○	○	○

6.
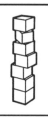

3	7	10	13
○	○	○	○

Math: Concepts/Applications—Problem Solving (Addition)

Sample

Mrs. Taylor planted 6 pink rose bushes and 5 white rose bushes in her front yard. Which number sentence tells how to find the number of rose bushes she planted altogether?

- ○ 5 + 1 = 6
- ○ 6 − 1 = 5
- ○ 6 − 5 = 1
- ○ 6 + 5 = 11

1. Maria bought 5 candy bars on Monday. On Wednesday she bought 3 more. How many candy bars did Maria buy in all?

- ○ 2
- ○ 5
- ○ 3
- ○ 8

2. Ron has 5 baseball cards, 7 football cards, and 2 soccer cards. How many sports cards does Ron have in all?

- ○ 7
- ○ 12
- ○ 9
- ○ 14

3. Lin and José were playing checkers. Lin won 6 games and José won 4 games. How many games did they play?

- ○ 10
- ○ 4
- ○ 6
- ○ 2

4. At the Springton Zoo Reptile House there are 11 lizards, 25 snakes, and 7 turtles. How many reptiles are there in all?

- ○ 34
- ○ 36
- ○ 43
- ○ 32

5. Gus bought 2 tickets to the high school play. The tickets cost $4 each. Which number sentence tells how to find out how much money Gus spent altogether?

- ○ 2 + 4 = 6
- ○ 6 − 4 = 2
- ○ 4 + 4 = 8
- ○ 8 − 4 = 4

6. In the morning there were seven crows on the old oak tree. In the afternoon eight more crows joined them. How many crows were in the old oak tree in all?

- ○ 7
- ○ 15
- ○ 8
- ○ 16

Math: Concepts/Applications—Problem Solving (Subtraction)

Sample

On the east side of Oak Tree Lane there are 12 houses. There are 9 houses on the west side. How many more houses are there on the east side?

○ 12   ○ 9
○ 3   ○ 5

1. On Sunday, 35 children were playing in the park. Then 14 of them went home. How many children were still playing?

   ○ 21   ○ 49
   ○ 11   ○ 14

2. Jesse bought a bat for $13. He paid for it with a $20 bill. How much change did he get back?

   ○ $4   ○ $5
   ○ $6   ○ $7

3. Fred colored 24 Easter eggs. He colored 12 of them yellow and 12 of them blue. Fred gave 18 of them away to his friends. Which number sentence tells how to find the number of Easter eggs he had left?

   ○ 24 + 18 = 42   ○ 24 – 18 = 6
   ○ 24 – 12 = 12   ○ 18 – 12 = 6

4. Martha set the dinner table for 9 people. Only 7 people were able to come for dinner. How many sets of silverware should Martha take off of the table?

   ○ 2   ○ 7
   ○ 5   ○ 9

5. A group of 12 people planned to pick up their tickets at the box office on the night of the big game. Only 8 of these people made it to the game, and 5 of them were late. How many tickets were left at the box office?

   ○ 12   ○ 8
   ○ 5   ○ 4

6. There were 55 students who tried out for the school play. Only 33 students got parts. Which number sentence tells how to find out how many students did not get parts?

   ○ 55 + 33 = 88   ○ 55 – 33 = 22
   ○ 33 + 33 = 66   ○ 55 – 10 = 45

Math: Concepts/Applications—Problem Solving (Multiplication)

Sample

The city planted two trees in front of each house on Main Street. There are 28 houses on Main Street between 2nd and 3rd Avenues. How many trees were planted on that part of Main Street?

- ○ 5
- ○ 28
- ○ 6
- ○ 56

1. Zach has been invited to 3 birthday parties. He wants to give 5 baseball cards to each person who is having a birthday. Which number sentence can be used to find out how many cards Zach should buy?

- ○ 5 + 3 = 8
- ○ 5 x 3 = 15
- ○ 5 – 3 = 2
- ○ 5 x 2 = 10

2. A train has 12 passenger cars, 2 dining cars, and 3 baggage cars. Each passenger car has 9 people in it. How many people are traveling on the train altogether?

- ○ 17
- ○ 24
- ○ 36
- ○ 108

3. Room 24 had a class party. There are 28 children in the class. How many cookies did they need in order to give 3 cookies to each student?

- ○ 24
- ○ 84
- ○ 28
- ○ 56

4. Mrs. Ray was setting up a science experiment. She placed two slides by each of the 16 microscopes on the desks. Which number sentence shows how to find the number of slides she placed on the desks?

- ○ 16 – 2 = 14
- ○ 16 + 2 = 18
- ○ 16 x 2 = 32
- ○ 16 ÷ 2 = 8

5. There are 14 teams in Benny's baseball league. There are 10 children on each team. Every team will play 20 games during the season. How many children belong to the league?

- ○ 120
- ○ 160
- ○ 140
- ○ 180

6. The students were getting ready for a banquet. They expected 48 people to attend. They placed 3 decorations on each of the 8 tables. How many decorations did they use in all?

- ○ 3
- ○ 8
- ○ 24
- ○ 48

Math: Concepts/Applications—Two-Step Problem Solving

Sample

The ages of the three children in the Ramirez family add up to 17. Charles, the oldest boy, is 10. Lupe, the middle child, is 6. How old is the baby?

   ○ 1   ○ 3
   ○ 2   ○ 4

1. Jeff has $4 to buy 2 bottles of ketchup for the class picnic. The ketchup costs $1.20 a bottle. How much money will Jeff have left after he buys the ketchup?

   ○ $1.20   ○ $2.40
   ○ $1.60   ○ $2.60

2. Della has 22 sports cards. She has 7 baseball cards and 8 football cards. The rest of the cards are soccer cards. How many soccer cards does Della have?

   ○ 7   ○ 8
   ○ 14   ○ 15

3. Chan made 17 origami frogs. He gave 5 to Lin and 3 to Maria. How many frogs did Chan have left?

   ○ 3   ○ 5
   ○ 8   ○ 9

4. Gary's allowance is $5 a week, and Shamika's is $4 a week. Over a period of 4 weeks, how much more money does Gary receive?

   ○ $5   ○ $3
   ○ $4   ○ $2

5. Marilyn and her family went on a vacation for 14 days. They spent 5 days in Germany and 4 days in Italy. They spent the rest of the time in France. How many days did they spend in France?

   ○ 10   ○ 5
   ○ 9   ○ 4

6. Javier saved $50 to buy new clothes for school. He bought a shirt for $14 and a pair of jeans for $12. How much money does Javier have left for shoes?

   ○ $24   ○ $38
   ○ $36   ○ $20

Math: Concepts/Applications—Estimation

Sample

Look at the price list below. About how much does a bunch of green onions cost?

Salad Vegetables

green onions/bunch	$.29
carrots/bunch	$.35
corn/4 ears	$.99

- ○ $.20
- ○ $.30
- ○ $.40
- ○ $.90

---

1. One place mat costs $1.95. About how much would 6 place mats cost?

   - ○ $2.00
   - ○ $6.00
   - ○ $12.00
   - ○ $20.00

---

2. A box measures 18 inches on each side. About how much ribbon would you need to go around the box once?

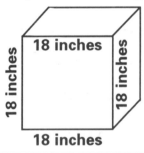

   - ○ 20 inches
   - ○ 40 inches
   - ○ 60 inches
   - ○ 80 inches

---

3. Read the shopping list. Which is the best way to figure out about how much all of the items on the list would cost?

Shopping List

1 half-gallon milk	$2.15
1 jar spaghetti sauce	$1.79
1 box of spaghetti	$ .99
1 package of meat	$2.79

   - ○ $2.00 + $1.00 + $0 + $2.00
   - ○ $2.00 + $2.00 + $1.00 + $3.00
   - ○ $1.00 + $1.00 + $1.00 + $2.00
   - ○ $2.00 + $7.00 + $9.00 + $2.00

Math: Concepts/Applications—Strategies

Sample

Suppose you had 2 jars full of buttons. Which answer shows the way to find the number of buttons altogether in both jars?

○ jar 1 + jar 2

○ jar 1 – jar 2

○ jar 1 x jar 2

○ jar 1 ÷ jar 2

1. How would you find the distance around this figure?

4 inches

3 inches

3 inches

6 inches

○ 4 in. + 6 in.

○ 4 in. x 6 in.

○ 4 in. + 6 in. + 3 in.

○ 4 in. + 3 in. + 6 in. + 3 in.

2. A pitcher holds 16 ounces of lemonade. You poured two 4-ounce glasses of lemonade for yourself and a friend. How could you find out how much is left in the pitcher?

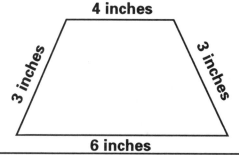

○ 16 ounces – 2 ounces

○ 16 ounces – 4 ounces

○ 16 ounces – 8 ounces

○ 16 ounces – 10 ounces

3. Read the shopping list. Which is the best way to figure out exactly how much all of the items on the list would cost?

Shopping List

1 half-gallon milk	$2.15
1 jar spaghetti sauce	$1.79
1 box of spaghetti	$ .99
1 package of meat	$2.79

○ add the dollar amounts only

○ add the cent amounts only

○ subtract the small amounts from the large ones

○ add all of the exact amounts

Math: Concepts/Applications—Reasonable Answers

Sample

About how high is a regular door?

- ○ 12 inches
- ○ 36 inches
- ○ 7 feet
- ○ 15 feet

1. About how long is an average-size car?

- ○ 1 foot
- ○ 1 yard
- ○ 10 feet
- ○ 25 feet

2. Pretend you are using a calculator to multiply 10 x 100. How many zeroes will be in the answer?

- ○ 1
- ○ 2
- ○ 3
- ○ 4

3. Imagine that you are setting the dinner table for 6 people. Each person will get 3 pieces of silverware: a knife, a fork, and a spoon. Which answer shows how many pieces of silverware you will need altogether?

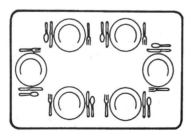

- ○ 3 x 1
- ○ 6 x 3
- ○ 3 x 6 x 3
- ○ 6 x 2

Teacher Scripts

> **NOTE:** The boxed information for each skill on the following pages references the Student Practice Pages (SPP).

Visual/Auditory Recognition: Letters

SPP 31

- Turn to page _____ in your test booklet. Find the number _____ at the top of the page and put your finger on it. (Check to see if everyone has found the number.)
- On this page you will find letters that I name. Look at the two samples at the top of the page. You will see a picture of a tree. Put your marker on the row with the tree.
- Look at the letters next to the tree. Who would like to name the letters? Now listen carefully. Which letter is the letter c? (the second letter) Fill in the circle under the letter c. Make sure you fill in the circle completely. Be sure the mark is dark.
- Move your marker to the row with the piggy bank. Look at the letters and listen carefully. Find the letter W. Which letter is the letter W? (the third letter) Fill in the circle under the third letter because it is the letter W.
- Now we will do the rest of the page. You are going to find more letters that I name. Listen carefully and look at the letters while you listen. Then fill in the circle under the letter I name.
- Move your marker to the row with the flowers. Mark the circle under the letter r . . . r.
- Move your marker to the row with the bunny. Mark the circle under the letter K . . . K.
- Move your marker to the row with the clover. Mark the circle under the letter j . . . j.
- Move your marker to the row with the lion. Mark the circle under the letter X . . . X.
- Move your marker to the row with the leaves. Mark the circle under the letter b . . . b.
- Move your marker to the row with the turtle. Mark the circle under the letter Q . . . Q.
- Move your marker to the row with the umbrella. Mark the circle under the letter e . . . e.

Visual/Auditory Recognition: Letters (Uppercase/Lowercase)

SPP 32

- Turn to page _____ in your test booklet. Find the number _____ at the top of the page and put your finger on it. (Check to see if everyone has found the number.)
- On this page you will find letters with the same names. Look at the two samples at the top of the page. You will see a picture of a tree. Put your marker on the row with the tree.
- Look at the letter in the box next to the tree. Who would like to name the letter? Now look at the other letters in the row. Which letter has the same name as the letter in the box? (the first letter) Yes, the letter in the box is capital E and the first letter is small e. Fill in the circle under the small e because it has the same name as the letter in the box.
- Move your marker to the row with the piggy bank. Look at the letter in the box. Who would like to name the letter? Now look at the other letters in the row. Which letter has the same name as the letter in the box? (the first letter) Yes, the letter in the box is small a and the first letter is capital A. Fill in the circle under the capital A because it has the same name as the letter in the box.
- Now you will do the rest of the page. Work by yourself. Look at the letter in the box. Then find the other letter with the same name. Mark the circle under that letter. Stop when you get to the bottom of the page.

Teacher Scripts

Recognition: Letters (in Words)

SPP 33

- Turn to page _____ in your test booklet. Find the number _____ at the top of the page and put your finger on it. (Check to see if everyone has found the number.)

- On this page you will find letters in words. Look at the two samples at the top of the page. You will see a picture of a tree. Put your marker on the row with the tree.

- Look at the letter in the box next to the tree. Who would like to name that letter? Now look at the words in the row. Which word has the letter that is in the box? (the first word) Yes, the letter in the box is c and the first word, cat, has the letter c in it. Fill in the circle under the first word because it has the letter in the box.

- Move your marker to the row with the piggy bank. Look at the letter in the box. Who would like to name that letter? Now look at the words in the row. Which word has the letter in the box? (the last word) Yes, the letter in the box is b and the last word, bed, has the letter b in it. Fill in the circle under the last word because it has the letter in the box.

- Now you will do the rest of the page. Work by yourself. Look at the letter in the box. Then find the word that has the same letter. Fill in the circle under that word. Stop when you get to the bottom of the page.

Recognition: Letter Groups and Words

SPP 34

- Turn to page _____ in your test booklet. Find the number _____ at the top of the page and put your finger on it. (Check to see if everyone has found the number.)

- On this page you will match letter groups and words. Look at the two samples at the top of the page. You should see a picture of a piggy bank. Put your marker on the row with the piggy bank. Look at the group of letters in the box. Look at the other letter groups in the row. Which group looks exactly the same as the group of letters in the box? (the third group) Yes, the third group of letters matches the letters in the box. Fill in the circle under the third group of letters.

- Move your marker to the row with the tree. Look at the group of letters in the box. Look at the other letter groups in the row. Which group looks exactly the same as the group of letters in the box? (the last group) Yes, the last group of letters matches the letters in the box. Fill in the circle under the last group of letters.

- Now you will do the rest of the page. Work by yourself. Look at the group of letters in the box. Then find the other group of letters that looks exactly the same. Fill in the circle under that group. Stop when you get to the bottom of the page.

Teacher Scripts

Visual/Auditory Recognition: Word Pairs

- Turn to page _____ in your test booklet. Find the number _____ at the top of the page and put your finger on it. (Check to see if everyone has found the number.)

- On this page you are going to decide if the words I say are the same or different. Look at the first sample at the top of the page. You will see a picture of a tree. Put your marker under the row with the tree.

- I will say two words. If the words I say are the same, fill in the circle under the two horses because they are the same. If the words I say are different, fill in the circle under the cow and the horse because those animals are different.

- Listen carefully. Here are the two words: street . . . street. Are the two words the same or are they different? (same) Yes, the words are the same. Which circle should you fill in? (the one under the two horses) Right. Fill in the circle under the two horses because they are the same.

- Move your marker to the row with the piggy bank. Listen carefully to the next two words: pot . . . pond. If they are the same, fill in the circle under the two horses. If they are different, fill in the circle under the cow and the horse. Listen again: pot . . . pond. Which circle did you fill in? You should have filled in the circle under the cow and the horse because the words I said were different.

- Move your marker to row 1. Listen to these two words: horse . . . house. If the words sound the same, fill in the circle under the two horses. If they sound different, fill in the circle under the cow and the horse. Horse . . . house.

- Move your marker to row 2. Listen to these two words: chair . . . chair. If the words sound the same, fill in the circle under the two horses. If they sound different, fill in the circle under the cow and the horse. Chair . . . chair.

- Move your marker to row 3. Listen to these words: swing . . . spring. If the words sound the same, fill in the circle under the two horses. If they sound different, fill in the circle under the cow and the horse. Swing . . . spring.

Word Analysis/Attack: Sight Words/Vocabulary

- Turn to page _____ in your test booklet. Find the number _____ at the top of the page and put your finger on it. (Check to see if everyone has found the number.)

- On this page you will match written words with the words I say. Put your marker under the sample with the tree. Look at the four words and listen carefully. Fill in the circle under the word boy . . . boy. Which word did you choose? (the second word) Yes, boy is the second word.

- Move your marker down under the second sample with the piggy bank. Look at the four words and listen carefully. Fill in the circle under the word now . . . now. Which word did you choose? (the third word) Yes, now is the third word.

- Move down to item 1. Fill in the circle under the word mother . . . mother.

- Move down to item 2. Fill in the circle under the word back . . . back.

- Move down to item 3. Fill in the circle under the word talk . . . talk.

- Move down to item 4. Fill in the circle under the word says . . . says.

- Move down to item 5. Fill in the circle under the word like . . . like.

- Move down to item 6. Fill in the circle under the word people . . . people.

- Move down to item 7. Fill in the circle under the word were . . . were.

Teacher Scripts

Word Analysis/Attack: Rhyming Sounds

- Turn to page _____ in your test booklet. Find the number _____ at the top of the page and put your finger on it. (Check to see if everyone has found the number.)

- On this page you will listen for rhyming words. Put your marker on the row with the tree. Look at the pictures in this row. Listen while I name the pictures: bear . . . bell . . . rain. Which word rhymes with chair? (bear) That's right. Bear rhymes with chair. Fill in the circle under the picture of the bear because bear and chair are rhyming words.

- Move your marker to row 1. Look at the pictures in this row. Listen while I name the pictures: pen . . . plane . . . fan. Which word rhymes with ran? Fill in the circle under the picture of the plane because plane and rain are rhyming words.

- Move your marker to row 2. Look at the pictures in this row. Listen while I name the pictures: bus . . . mat . . . ring. Which word rhymes with king? Fill in the circle under the picture of something that rhymes with king.

- Move your marker to row 3. Look at the pictures in this row. Listen while I name the pictures: dog . . . boy . . . ghost. Which word rhymes with frog? Fill in the circle under the picture of something that rhymes with frog.

- Move your marker to row 4. Look at the pictures in this row. Listen while I name the pictures: jar . . . rooster . . . cup. Which word rhymes with car? Fill in the circle under the picture of something that rhymes with car.

- Move your marker to row 5. Look at the pictures in this row. Listen while I name the pictures: cake . . . book . . . house. Which word rhymes with hook? Fill in the circle under the picture of something that rhymes with hook.

- Move your marker to row 6. Look at the pictures in this row. Listen while I name the pictures: dish . . . shoe . . . fan. Which word rhymes with fish? Fill in the circle under the picture of something that rhymes with fish.

Teacher Scripts

Word Analysis/Attack: Beginning Sounds

- Turn to page _____ in your test booklet. Find the number _____ at the top of the page and put your finger on it. (Check to see if everyone has found the number.)

- On this page you will match the beginning sounds of words. Put your marker on the row with the tree. Look at the pictures in this row. Listen while I name the pictures: cat . . . dog . . . egg. Which word has the same beginning sound as dinosaur? (dog) That's right, dog begins with the same sound as dinosaur. Fill in the circle under the picture of the dog because dog and dinosaur begin with the same sound.

- Move your marker to row 1. Look at the pictures in this row. Listen while I name the pictures: bell . . . fish . . . plant. Which word has the same beginning sound as play? Fill in the circle under the picture with the same beginning sound as play.

- Move your marker to row 2. Look at the pictures in this row. Listen while I name the pictures: web . . . saw . . . lock. Which word has the same beginning sound as ladder? Fill in the circle under the picture with the same beginning sound as ladder.

- Move your marker to row 3. Look at the pictures in this row. Listen while I name the pictures: sandwich . . . tent . . . shell. Which word has the same beginning sound as shoe? Fill in the circle under the picture with the same beginning sound as shoe.

- Move your marker to row 4. Look at the pictures in this row. Listen while I name the pictures: key . . . flower . . . truck. Which word has the same beginning sound as tree? Fill in the circle under the picture with the same beginning sound as tree.

- Move your marker to row 5. Look at the pictures in this row. Listen while I name the pictures: ring . . . vase . . . lion. Which word has the same beginning sound as van? Fill in the circle under the picture with the same beginning sound as van.

- Move your marker to row 6. Look at the pictures in this row. Listen while I name the pictures: carrot . . . mask . . . rabbit. Which word has the same beginning sound as castle? Fill in the circle under the picture with the same beginning sound as castle.

Teacher Scripts

Word Analysis/Attack: Ending Sounds

- Turn to page _____ in your test booklet. Find the number _____ at the top of the page and put your finger on it. (Check to see if everyone has found the number.)

- On this page you will match the ending sounds of words. Put your marker on the row with the tree. Look at the pictures in this row. Listen while I name the pictures: chair . . . feet . . . corncob. Which word has the same ending sound as four? (chair) That's right, chair ends with the same sound as four. Fill in the circle under the picture of the chair because chair and four end with the same sound.

- Move your marker to row 1. Look at the pictures in this row. Listen while I name the pictures: bird . . . peach . . . chin. Fill in the circle under the picture of the peach because peach and ranch end with the same sound.

- Move your marker to row 2. Look at the pictures in this row. Listen while I name the pictures: man . . . pin . . . fox. Which word has the same ending sound as mix? Fill in the circle under the picture with the same ending sound as mix.

- Move your marker to row 3. Look at the pictures in this row. Listen while I name the pictures: shell . . . pie . . . soap. Which word has the same ending sound as ship? Fill in the circle under the picture with the same ending sound as ship.

- Move your marker to row 4. Look at the pictures in this row. Listen while I name the pictures: door . . . fence . . . apple. Which word has the same ending sound as far? Fill in the circle under the picture with the same ending sound as far.

- Move your marker to row 5. Look at the pictures in this row. Listen while I name the pictures: car . . . bike . . . fan. Which word has the same ending sound as cake? Fill in the circle under the picture with the same ending sound as cake.

- Move your marker to row 6. Look at the pictures in this row. Listen while I name the pictures: egg . . . bird . . . truck. Which word has the same ending sound as cord? Fill in the circle under the picture with the same ending sound as cord.

Teacher Scripts

Word Analysis/Attack: Beginning Consonants

SPP 39

- Turn to page _____ in your test booklet. Find the number _____ at the top of the page and put your finger on it. (Check to see if everyone has found the number.)
- On this page you will match the beginning sounds of words. Put your marker under the row with the tree. Who will read the four words on this row? Now listen carefully. Which word begins with the same sound as the word bat . . . bat? (bell) Yes, bell has the same beginning sound as bat. Fill in the circle under the word bell because bat and bell begin with the same sound.
- Move your marker to the row with the piggy bank. Look at the four words. Read the words to yourself. Now listen carefully. Which word begins with the same sound as the word pony . . . pony? (pan) Yes, fill in the circle under the word pan because pan has the same beginning sound as pony.
- Move your marker to the row with the flowers. Look at the four words. Fill in the circle under the word that begins with the same sound as now . . . now.
- Move your marker to the row with the bunny. Look at the four words. Fill in the circle under the word that begins with the same sound as kite . . . kite.
- Move your marker to the row with the clover. Look at the four words. Fill in the circle under the word that begins with the same sound as rat . . . rat.
- Move your marker to the row with the lion. Look at the four words. Fill in the circle under the word that begins with the same sound as jam . . . jam.
- Move your marker to the row with the leaves. Look at the three words. Fill in the circle under the word that begins with the same sound as there . . . there.
- Move your marker to the row with the turtle. Look at the three words. Fill in the circle under the word that begins with the same sound as cry . . . cry.
- Move your marker to the row with the umbrella. Look at the three words. Fill in the circle under the word that begins with the same sound as shut . . . shut.

Word Analysis/Attack: Ending Consonants

SPP 40

- Turn to page _____ in your test booklet. Find the number _____ at the top of the page and put your finger on it. (Check to see if everyone has found the number.)
- On this page you will match the ending sounds of words. Put your marker under the row with the tree. Who will read the four words in this row? Now listen carefully. Which word ends with the same sound as the word tug . . . tug? (log) Yes, log has the same ending sound as tug. Fill in the circle under the word log because tug and log end with the same sound.
- Move your marker to the row with the piggy bank. Read the four words to yourself. Now listen carefully. Which word ends with the same sound as the word think . . . think? (tank) Yes. Fill in the circle under the word tank because tank has the same ending sound as think.
- Move your marker to the row with the flowers. Look at the four words. Fill in the circle under the word that ends with the same sound as dip . . . dip.
- Move your marker to the row with the bunny. Look at the four words. Fill in the circle under the word that ends with the same sound as fan . . . fan.
- Move your marker to the row with the clover. Look at the four words. Fill in the circle under the word that ends with the same sound as bag . . . bag.
- Move your marker to the row with the lion. Look at the three words. Fill in the circle under the word that ends with the same sound as send . . . send.
- Move your marker to the row with the leaves. Look at the three words. Fill in the circle under the word that ends with the same sound as fish . . . fish.
- Move your marker to the row with the turtle. Look at the three words. Fill in the circle under the word that ends with the same sound as found . . . found.
- Move your marker to the row with the umbrella. Look at the three words. Fill in the circle under the word that ends with the same sound as bolt . . . bolt.

Teacher Scripts

Word Analysis/Attack: Consonant Substitutions

- Turn to page _____ in your test booklet. Find the number _____ at the top of the page and put your finger on it. (Check to see if everyone has found the number.)
- On this page you find beginning letters for words. Put your marker in the row with the tree. The name of the first picture is king. Under the picture of the king is the letter r. Now listen carefully. Take away the k at the beginning of the word king and put the r in its place. What word does it make? (ring) Now look at the three pictures next to the king. Which picture matches the new word you made? (the first picture) Yes, the name of the first picture is ring. When you take away the k from the word king and put the letter r in its place, you make the word ring. Fill in the circle under the picture of the ring.
- Move your marker to the row with the piggy bank. This is another kind of item. Look at the picture of a book. Look at the letters underneath the picture. What letter goes in front of o-o-k to spell book? (b) Fill in the circle under the letter b because b-o-o-k spells book.
- Move your marker to row 1. Look at the picture of a can. Can begins with c. Take away the c and put an f in its place. Look at the three pictures in the row with the can. Fill in the circle under the one that shows the new word.
- Move your marker to row 2. Look at the picture of a jar. Jar begins with j. Take away the j and put a c in its place. Look at the three pictures in the row next to the jar. Fill in the circle under the one that shows the new word.
- Move your marker to row 3. Look at the picture of a boat. Boat begins with b. Take away the b and put a g in its place. Look at the three pictures in the row next to the boat. Fill in the circle under the one that shows the new word.
- Move your marker to row 4. Look at the picture of a dog. Fill in the circle under the letter you would put at the beginning of o-g to spell dog.
- Move your marker to row 5. Look at the picture of a swing. Fill in the circle under the letters you would put at the beginning of i-n-g to spell swing.
- Move your marker to row 6. Look at the picture of a chair. Fill in the circle under the letters you would put at the beginning of a-i-r to spell chair.

Word Analysis/Attack: Silent Letters

- Turn to page _____ in your test booklet. Find the number _____ at the top of the page and put your finger on it. (Check to see if everyone has found the number.)
- On this page you will find words with silent letters in them. Put your marker on the first sample with the tree. Who will read the words in this row? One word has a letter that is silent, or not sounded. Which one is it? (sword) The first word, sword, has a silent letter, the w. Fill in the circle under the word sword.
- Move your marker to the second sample with the piggy bank. Read the words to yourself. One word has a letter that is silent, or not sounded. Which one is it? (write) The second word, write, has a silent letter, the w. Fill in the circle under the word write.
- Do the rest of the page by yourself in the same way that you did the samples. Find the word with the silent letter in each row and fill in the circle underneath it.

Teacher Scripts

Word Analysis/Attack: Vowel Sounds

- Turn to page _____ in your test booklet. Find the number _____ at the top of the page and put your finger on it. (Check to see if everyone has found the number.)

- On this page you will match vowel sounds. Put your marker under the two sample questions at the top of the page. They are marked with small arrows. Look at the first sample. You will see the word cat with a line under the letter a. Think about the sound of the a in cat. (It is called a "short" a sound.) Now look at the three words below the word cat. Which word has the same vowel sound as cat? (sand) The word sand has the same vowel sound as cat. Fill in the circle under the word sand.

- Look across the top of the page at the other sample question. You will see the word cake with a line under the a. Think about the vowel sound of the a in cake. (It is called a "long" a sound.) Now look at the three words below the word cake. Which word has the same vowel sound as cake? (made) Fill in the circle under the word made.

- Move your marker to the first set of words in the first column where you see the number 1 and the balloon. Which word has the same sound as the underlined letter in pot . . . pot? Fill in the circle.

- Move your marker to the next row where you see the number 2 and the bear. Which word has the same sound as the underlined letter in met . . . met? Fill in the circle.

- Move your marker to the next row where you see the number 3 and the apple. Which word has the same sound as the underlined letter in slip . . . slip? Fill in the circle.

- Move your marker to the next row where you see the number 4 and the grapes. Which word has the same sound as the underlined letter in map . . . map? Fill in the circle.

- Move your marker to the next row where you see the number 5 and the flag. Which word has the same sound as the underlined letter in duck . . . duck? Fill in the circle.

- Move your marker to the next row where you see the number 6 and the key. Which word has the same sound as the underlined letter in make . . . make? Fill in the circle.

- Move your marker to the next row where you see the number 7 and the cup. Which word has the same sound as the underlined letters in see . . . see? Fill in the circle.

- Now move your marker up to the set of words near the top of the second column where you see the number 8 and the schoolgirl. Which word has the same sound as the underlined letter in like . . . like? Fill in the circle.

- Move your marker to the next row where you see the number 9 and the books. Which word has the same sound as the underlined letter in told . . . told? Fill in the circle.

- Move your marker to the next row where you see the number 10 and the schoolboy. Which word has the same sound as the underlined letter in use . . . use? Fill in the circle.

- Move your marker to the next row where you see the number 11 and the calculator. Which word has the same sound as the underlined letters in crown . . . crown? Fill in the circle.

- Move your marker to the next row where you see the number 12 and the ladder. Which word has the same sound as the underlined letters in cause . . . cause? Fill in the circle.

- Move your marker to the next row where you see the number 13 and the paintbrush. Which word has the same sound as the underlined letters in clown . . . clown? Fill in the circle.

- Move your marker to the next row where you see the number 14 and the star. Which word has the same sound as the underlined letters in toy . . . toy? Fill in the circle.

Teacher Scripts

Word Analysis/Attack: Compound Words

SPP 45

- Turn to page _____ in your test booklet. Find the number _____ at the top of the page and put your finger on it. (Check to see if everyone has found the number.)
- On this page you will find words that are made up of two words. These words are called <u>compound words</u>. Put your marker under the sample question by the tree at the top of the page. Look at the four words in the row. Who can read these words for us? Which word is made up of two words that can stand alone? (football) What are the words? (foot and ball) Fill in the circle under the word football because football is a compound word.
- Work by yourself on the rest of the page. Find the compound word in each row. Choose only one answer for each question. Fill in the circle under each compound word.

Word Analysis/Attack: Contractions

SPP 46

- Turn to page _____ in your test booklet. Find the number _____ at the top of the page and put your finger on it. (Check to see if everyone has found the number.)
- On this page you will match words called <u>contractions</u> to the pairs of words that mean the same thing. Put your marker in the sample section at the top of the page. The first word that is underlined is a contraction. Who can read the underlined word for us? (isn't) Now read the four pairs of words in same row. (is none, is not, is net, is nothing) Which two words have the same meaning as isn't? (is not) Fill in the circle under is not because is not has the same meaning as isn't.
- Work by yourself on the rest of the page. In each row, find the two words that have the same meaning as the underlined contraction and fill in the circle under your choice.

Word Analysis/Attack: Root Words

SPP 47

- Turn to page _____ in your test booklet. Find the number _____ at the top of the page and put your finger on it. (Check to see if everyone has found the number.)
- On this page you will find <u>root words</u>. A root word is the same as a base word. Can anyone tell us what a root word is? (a word to which a prefix or a suffix is added to make another word) Look at the first sample by the tree at the top of the page. The first word, unhappy, is underlined. What is the root word of unhappy? (happy) Look at the four answer choices and fill in the circle under happy because happy is the root word of unhappy.
- Move down to the next sample by the piggy bank. The first word, slowest, is underlined. What is the root word of slowest? (slow) Look at the four answer choices and fill in the circle under slow because slow is the root word of slowest.
- Work by yourself on the rest of the page. In each row, find the root word of the underlined word and fill in the circle under your choice.

Word Analysis/Attack: Prefixes

SPP 48

- Turn to page _____ in your test booklet. Find the number _____ at the top of the page and put your finger on it. (Check to see if everyone has found the number.)
- On this page you will find <u>prefixes</u>. A prefix is one or more letters added to the beginning of a word to make a different word. Look at the sample by the tree at the top of the page. Who can read the underlined word? (underground) Now look at the four answer choices. Which one is the prefix of the word underground? (under) Fill in the circle under the second answer choice, under, because it is the prefix in the word underground.
- Work by yourself on the rest of the page. In each row, find the prefix of the underlined word and fill in the circle under your choice.

Teacher Scripts

Word Analysis/Attack: Suffixes

- Turn to page _____ in your test booklet. Find the number _____ at the top of the page and put your finger on it. (Check to see if everyone has found the number.)
- On this page you will find <u>suffixes</u>. A suffix is one or more letters added to the end of a word to make a different word. Look at the sample by the tree at the top of the page. Who can read the first word, the underlined word? (certainly) Now look at the four answer choices. Which one is the suffix of the word certainly? (ly) Fill in the circle under the second answer choice, ly, because it is the suffix in the word certainly.
- Work by yourself on the rest of the page. In each row, find the suffix of the underlined word and fill in the answer circle under your choice.

Word Analysis/Attack: Inflectional Endings

- Turn to page _____ in your test booklet. Find the number _____ at the top of the page and put your finger on it. (Check to see if everyone has found the number.)
- On this page you will find the word I say. Put your marker under sample A at the top of the page. In sample A there are three words: walk . . . walking . . . walks. First, I will say one of the words. Then I will use it in a sentence. You will find the word I say. Listen carefully. Find the word walking. The boys are walking. Walking. Which word did you choose? (second) The second word is the right choice because it is walking. Fill in the circle next to the second word.
- Look across the top of the page at sample B. There are three words: brighter . . . brightest . . . brightly. First, I will say one of the words. Then I will use it in a sentence. You will find the word I say. Listen carefully. Find the word brightest. That light is the brightest. Brightest. Which word did you choose? (second) The second word is the right choice because it is brightest. Fill in the circle next to the second word.
- Move your marker to the first set of words in the first column where you see the number 1 and the balloon. Fill in the circle next to runs. He runs very fast. Runs.
- Move your marker to the next set of words where you see the number 2 and the teddy bear. Fill in the circle next to nicest. This is the nicest picture. Nicest.
- Move your marker to the next set of words where you see the number 3 and the apple. Fill in the circle next to painted. She painted it yesterday. Painted.
- Move your marker to the next set of words where you see the number 4 and the grapes. Fill in the circle next to happier. She is happier because she found her homework. Happier.
- Move your marker up to almost the top of the second column where you see the number 5 and the schoolgirl. Fill in the circle next to hopped. He hopped on one foot. Hopped.
- Move your marker to the next set of words where you see the number 6 and the books. Fill in the circle next to neatly. Do your work neatly. Neatly.
- Move your marker to the next set of words where you see the number 7 and the schoolboy. Fill in the circle next to mailing. Did he forget about mailing the letter? Mailing.
- Move your marker to the next set of words where you see the number 8 and the calculator. Fill in the circle next to shouting. What is all the shouting about? Shouting.

Teacher Scripts

Word Analysis/Attack: Syllables

SPP 51

- Turn to page _____ in your test booklet. Find the number _____ at the top of the page and put your finger on it. (Check to see if everyone has found the number.)

- On this page you will find the number of syllables in words. Syllables are the parts of a word you hear when you say the word. Look at the sample by the tree. Who can read the underlined word? (beautiful) How many syllables do you hear in the word beautiful? (three) Look at the numerals given as answer choices. Fill in the circle under the numeral three to show that beautiful has three syllables.

- Work by yourself on the rest of the page. In each row, find the number of syllables in the underlined word and fill in the answer circle under your choice.

Word Analysis/Attack: Endings/Compounds

SPP 52

- Turn to page _____ in your test booklet. Find the number _____ at the top of the page and put your finger on it. (Check to see if everyone has found the number.)

- On this page you will find endings that can be added to words to make new words. You will also find pairs of words that can be put together to make new words. Look at sample A. Read the word in the box. (walk) Now look at the three endings next to the word walk. Let's read the word walk aloud with each of the three endings added to it to see which one makes a real new word. (walkest, walkly, walking) Which ending makes a new word when it is added to walk? (ing) Fill in the answer circle under the ending ing to show that ing can be added to walk to make the new word walking.

- Look at sample B. Each answer has a pair of words. Let's read the two words in each pair as if they were one word. Do they all sound like real words? (yes) Now look at how the words in each pair are spelled. Which two words make a correctly spelled new word when they are put together? (foot and ball) Fill in the first answer circle to show that foot and ball make a correctly spelled word when they are put together.

- Move your marker to the first set of words in the first column where you see the number 1 and the balloon. Fill in the circle under the ending that makes a new word when it is added to trust.

- Move your marker to the next set of words where you see the number 2 and the bear. Fill in the circle under the ending that makes a new word when it is added to danger.

- Move your marker to the next set of words where you see the number 3 and the apple. Fill in the circle under the ending that makes a new word when it is added to forget.

- Move your marker to the next set of words where you see the number 4 and the grapes. Fill in the circle under the ending that makes a new word when it is added to friend.

- Move your marker to the top of the next column where you see the number 5 and the schoolgirl. Fill in the circle under the two words that make a correctly spelled new word when they are put together.

- Do the rest of the page the same way you did number 5. Work by yourself until you come to the end of the page.

Teacher Scripts

Vocabulary: Pictures (1)

SPP 53

- Turn to page _____ in your test booklet. Find the number _____ at the top of the page and put your finger on it. (Check to see if everyone has found the number.)
- On this page you will find words that match pictures. Look at the sample. What does the picture show. (a girl sitting at a desk) Now look at the words. Who can read them for us? Which word best tells what the picture shows? (girl) Fill in the circle under girl because girl goes best with the picture.
- Work by yourself on the rest of the page. First look at the picture. Then read the four answer choices. Fill in the circle under the word that best tells about the picture.

Vocabulary: Pictures (2)

SPP 54

- Turn to page _____ in your test booklet. Find the number _____ at the top of the page and put your finger on it. (Check to see if everyone has found the number.)
- On this page you will choose a picture to fill in the blank or to go with a sentence I will say. Look at the sample. Look at the pictures while you listen to this sentence: "You can put your money in a (blank) . . . You can put your money in a (blank)." Fill in the circle under the picture that shows what word is missing from the sentence. (pause) You should have filled in the circle under the first picture, the piggy bank. The completed sentence should be: "You can put your money in a piggy bank."
- Find number 1. Look at the pictures. "The rider put a saddle on the (blank) . . . The rider put a saddle on the (blank). Mark your answer. (pause)
- Find number 2. Look at the pictures. Find the picture of "the cup beside the table . . . the cup beside the table." Mark your answer. (pause)
- Find number 3. Look at the pictures. "We rode a (blank) at the birthday party . . . We rode a (blank) at the birthday party." Mark your answer. (pause)
- Find number 4. Look at the pictures. Find the picture of "something to use on a hot day . . . something to use on a hot day." Mark your answer. (pause)

Vocabulary: Word Categories

SPP 55

- Turn to page _____ in your test booklet. Find the number _____ at the top of the page and put your finger on it. (Check to see if everyone has found the number.)
- On this page you will choose a picture to go with what I describe. Look at the sample. Look at the three pictures and listen carefully. Which picture shows a tool . . . a tool? (the third picture, a saw) A saw is a tool. Fill in the answer circle under the picture of the saw because a saw is a tool.
- Put your marker on number 1. Fill in the circle under the picture that shows something hot . . . something hot.
- Move your marker to number 2. Fill in the circle under the picture that shows something that makes a noise . . . something that makes a noise.
- Move your marker to number 3. Fill in the circle under the picture that shows something to wear . . . something to wear.
- Move your marker to the number 4. Fill in the circle under the picture that shows something indoors . . . something indoors.
- Move your marker to the number 5. Fill in the circle under the picture that shows a place for people . . . a place for people.
- Move your marker to the number 6. Fill in the circle under the picture that shows something to eat . . . something to eat.

Teacher Scripts

Vocabulary: Word Categories (and Meanings)

SPP 56

- Turn to page _____ in your test booklet. Find the number _____ at the top of the page and put your finger on it. (Check to see if everyone has found the number.)

- On this page you will choose words to go with the categories and meanings I read to you. Find the first sample by the tree. Read the four words. Which word is used to tell about the weather . . . to tell about the weather? (rainy) Fill in the answer circle under the word rainy because it is a word that is used to tell about the weather.

- Now look at the second sample by the piggy bank. Read the four words in that row. Which word fits the meaning to move very fast . . . to move very fast? (run) Fill in the circle under the word run because run means to move very fast.

- Now find the number 1 and the flowers. Fill in the circle under the word that is a kind of pet . . . a pet.

- Now find the number 2 and the bunny. Fill in the circle under the word that is the name of a meal . . . a meal.

- Find the number 3 and the clover. Fill in the circle under the word that is the name of something that shines . . . something that shines.

- Find the number 4 and the lion. Fill in the circle under the word that is the name of a flower . . . a flower.

- Find the number 5 and the leaves. Fill in the circle under the word that is the name of a place to borrow books . . . a place to borrow books.

- Find the number 6 and the turtle. Fill in the circle under the word that is the name of a place for cars to drive . . . a place for cars to drive.

- Find the number 7 and the umbrella. Fill in the circle under the word that fits the meaning not tall . . . not tall.

Vocabulary: Word Categories (Does Not Belong)

SPP 57

- Turn to page _____ in your test booklet. Find the number _____ at the top of the page and put your finger on it. (Check to see if everyone has found the number.)

- On this page you will find words that do not go together. Look at the sample by the tree. Read the four words in that row. One word does not go together with the other words. Which word is it? (carrot) Why? (All of the other words have something to do with playing baseball; carrot is the only word that is not a baseball word.) Fill in the circle under carrot because carrot does not go with the other words.

- Now finish the rest of the page by yourself in the same way we did the sample. In each row find the one word that does not go with the other words. Fill in the circle for your choice.

Teacher Scripts

Vocabulary: Words with Similar Meanings (Synonyms)   ☐ SPP 58

- Turn to page _____ in your test booklet. Find the number _____ at the top of the page and put your finger on it. (Check to see if everyone has found the number.)
- On this page you will find words that have the same or almost the same meanings as other words. Look at sample A. Read the phrase. Which word is underlined? (large) Now read the words under the phrase. You can have a small glass of milk, a big glass of milk, or a cold glass of milk so you have to think about the meaning of the word large to find the right answer. Which word means the same or almost the same as large? (big) Fill in the circle in front of big because big has the same meaning as large.
- Now look at sample B. Read the phrase to yourself and think about the meaning of the underlined word. Then read the three words under the phrase. Which word in the phrase is underlined? (bake) Which word means the same or almost the same as bake? (cook) Fill in the circle in front of the word cook.
- Now finish the rest of the page by yourself in the same way that we did the samples. In each item find the word that means the same or almost the same as the underlined word in the phrase. Fill in the circle by your answer choice.

Vocabulary: Words with Opposite Meanings (Antonyms)   ☐ SPP 59

- Turn to page _____ in your test booklet. Find the number _____ at the top of the page and put your finger on it. (Check to see if everyone has found the number.)
- On this page you will find words that have opposite meanings from the words underlined in the phrases. Look at sample A. Read the phrase. Which word is underlined? (hot) Now read the words under the phrase. Find the word that has the opposite meaning of the underlined word, hot. (cold) Fill in the circle in front of the word cold because cold is the opposite of hot.
- Now look at sample B. Read the phrase to yourself and think about the meaning of the underlined word. Then read the answer choices under the phrase. Fill in the circle in front of the answer that has the opposite meaning of the underlined word in the phrase. You should have marked the second choice, begin, because begin is the opposite of end.
- Now finish the rest of the page by yourself in the same way that we did the samples. In each item find the word that is the opposite of the underlined word in the phrase. Fill in the circle by your answer choice.

Vocabulary: Suffix Meanings   ☐ SPP 60

- Turn to page _____ in your test booklet. Find the number _____ at the top of the page and put your finger on it. (Check to see if everyone has found the number.)
- On this page you will find the meanings of suffixes. Look at sample A. Read the two words at the top of the box. What are the underlined letters in each word? (ian) Now read the answer choices. What does the suffix ian in each word mean? (person from) A Washingtonian is a person from Washington, and a Houstonian is a person from Houston. Fill in the circle in front of the words person from.
- Look at sample B. Read the two words at the top of the box. What are the underlined letters in each word? (ist) Now read the answer choices. What does the suffix ist in each word mean? (person who) A guitarist is a person who plays the guitar, and a pianist is a person who plays the piano. Fill in the circle in front of the words person who.
- Now finish the rest of the page by yourself in the same way that we did the samples. In each item choose the answer that tells the meaning of the underlined suffix. Fill in the circle by your answer choice.

Teacher Scripts

Vocabulary: Word Part Clues

SPP 61

- Turn to page _____ in your test booklet. Find the number _____ at the top of the page and put your finger on it. (Check to see if everyone has found the number.)
- On this page you will find the right words to complete the sentences. Find the balloon in sample A. Read the sentence with a missing word and the answer choices below it. The answer choices look very much alike. Which word fits best in the sentence? (unhappy) What is the complete sentence? (She was unhappy because she broke her toy.) Why are the other answer choices not as good? (They are not real words.) Fill in the answer circle next to unhappy because it fits best in the sentence.
- Find the schoolgirl in sample B. Read the sentence and the answer choices to yourself. Look carefully at all of the answer choices to find the one that makes the most sense in the sentence. Which word fits best in the sentence? (reading) Fill in the circle next to reading.
- Now finish the rest of the page by yourself in the same way that we did the samples. In each item choose the word that fits best in the sentence. Fill in the circle by your answer choice.

Vocabulary: Multiple Meanings Words (Definitions)

SPP 62

- Turn to page _____ in your test booklet. Find the number _____ at the top of the page and put your finger on it. (Check to see if everyone has found the number.)
- On this page you will find words that have two meanings. Look at the sample by the tree. There are two underlined word meanings. Both are for the same word. Read the first meaning. Read the second meaning. Now read the four words underneath the meanings. Which word can mean something to wear and short, quick breaths? (pants) Fill in the circle by the word pants.
- Now finish the rest of the page by yourself in the same way that we did the sample. In each item choose the word that works with both of the meanings. Fill in the circle by your answer choice.

Vocabulary: Multiple Meanings (in Sentences)

SPP 63

- Turn to page _____ in your test booklet. Find the number _____ at the top of the page and put your finger on it. (Check to see if everyone has found the number.)
- On this page you will find words that have more than one meaning. Look at the sample by the tree. There is a word missing in each sentence. The word that is missing fits in both sentences. Read the two sentences. Then read the four answer choices. Which word fits in both sentences? (fair) Yes, to play fair is to obey the rules, and a fair is an event with rides. Fill in the circle in front of the word fair.
- Now finish the rest of the page by yourself in the same way that we did the sample. In each item choose the word that fits in both of the sentences. Fill in the circle by your answer choice.

Vocabulary: Words in Context

SPP 64

- Turn to page _____ in your test booklet. Find the number _____ at the top of the page and put your finger on it. (Check to see if everyone has found the number.)
- On this page you will find words that fit in blanks in sentences and paragraphs. Look at sample A. Read the story and look at the words below it. Which word fits best in the blank in the story? (tired) The complete story is The play was very long. The actors were tired. Fill in the circle beside tired.
- Do sample B by yourself. Which word fits correctly in the blank? (called) Called is correct. Fill in the circle beside called.
- Now finish the rest of the page by yourself in the same way that we did the samples. In each item choose the word that fits correctly in each blank. Fill in the circle by your answer choice.

Teacher Scripts

Reading Comprehension: Listening (Stories)

- Turn to page _____ in your test booklet. Find the number _____ at the top of the page and put your finger on it. (Check to see if everyone has found the number.)

- On this page you will listen to stories, and then you will find pictures that show the answers to questions I will ask about the stories. You will hear each question only once, so listen carefully.

- Put your marker on the sample by the tree. Look at the three pictures in the sample. I am going to read a story to you. Then I will ask you a question about the story.

     Donald looked at some toys in the toy store. He liked the game and the ball, but he decided to buy the drum.

- Now listen to the question. <u>Which toy did Donald decide to buy?</u> (the drum) Which picture shows the answer to the question? (the second one) Fill in the answer circle under the second picture because it shows which toy Donald decided to buy.

- Move your marker to the row marked number 1. Listen carefully to the story. This time, I will ask you more than one question at the end of the story.

     Elephants are the largest animals that live on land. They all have long trunks and sharp tusks made of ivory. Elephants live in both Asia and Africa. Asian elephants have small ears. African elephants have really big ears. Both kinds of elephants are very strong.

- Look at the three pictures. <u>What is the story mainly about?</u> Fill in the circle under the picture that shows what the story is mainly about.

- Move your marker to the row marked number 2. Look at the three pictures. <u>What do all elephants have?</u> Fill in the circle under the picture that shows what all elephants have.

- Move your marker to the row marked number 3. Listen carefully to the story. I will ask you more than one question about it at the end.

     Sally and her family went on a trip by car. They stayed in hotels and ate in restaurants. They had many good things to eat, but Sally's favorite was always pizza. Toward the end of the trip, they stayed near the beach for three days. They had a wonderful vacation.

- Look at the three pictures. <u>How did Sally and her family travel?</u> Fill in the circle under the picture that shows how Sally and her family traveled.

- Move your marker to the row marked number 4. Look at the three pictures. <u>What food did Sally like the best?</u> Fill in the circle under the picture that shows what food Sally liked the best.

- Move your marker to the row marked number 5. Look at the three pictures. <u>Where did Sally and her family stay for three days?</u> Fill in the circle under the picture that shows where Sally and her family stayed for three days.

Teacher Scripts

Reading Comprehension: Listening (Sentences)

SPP 65

- Turn to page _____ in your test booklet. Find the number _____ at the top of the page and put your finger on it. (Check to see if everyone has found the number.)

- On this page you will find pictures that match sentences. Find the sample by the tree. Put your marker under it. Look at the three pictures in the sample. Listen carefully to the sentence I will read to you. Look at the pictures as you listen. A cat sleeps under the table . . . A cat sleeps under the table. Which picture shows a cat sleeping under a table? (the second picture) The second picture shows what the sentence says. Fill in the circle under the second picture because it shows a cat sleeping under a table.

- Move your marker to the row marked number 1. Look at the three pictures in the row. Listen carefully to the sentence I will read to you. Look at the pictures as you listen. The birds are flying . . . the birds are flying. Fill in the circle under the picture that shows the birds are flying.

- Move your marker to the row marked number 2. Fill in the circle under the picture that shows this sentence: The girl is wearing a scarf . . . the girl is wearing a scarf.

- Move your marker to the row marked number 3. Fill in the circle under the picture that shows this sentence: The frog is on the rock . . . the frog is on the rock.

- Move your marker to the row marked number 4. Fill in the circle under the picture that shows this sentence: The girl is playing with a ball . . . the girl is playing with a ball.

- Move your marker to the row marked number 5. Fill in the circle under the picture that shows this sentence: The man is under the umbrella . . . the man is under the umbrella.

Reading Comprehension: Sentences (1 Picture/3 Sentences)

SPP 67

- Turn to page _____ in your test booklet. Find the number _____ at the top of the page and put your finger on it. (Check to see if everyone has found the number.)

- On this page you will choose the correct sentence to go with each picture. Look at the sample. You should see a picture and some sentences next to the picture. What does the picture show? (elicit descriptions) Now read the sentences. Find the sentence that best tells what the picture is about. The board has a hole in it tells the most about this picture. Fill in the answer circle next to this sentence: The board has a hole in it.

- Work by yourself on the rest of the page. Look at each picture. Then read the sentences next to the picture. Fill in the answer circle for the sentence that tells about the picture.

Teacher Scripts

Reading Comprehension: Word Recognition

- Turn to page _____ in your test booklet. Find the number _____ at the top of the page and put your finger on it. (Check to see if everyone has found the number.)

- On this page you will find words that match the words that I say. Put your marker under the sample A section. Look at the words in sample A. I will say the *key* word. That is the word you will look for. Then I will use the same word in a sentence. Listen carefully. The key word is light. Please turn on the light. Which word is the word light . . . light? (the third word) The third word is light. Fill in the circle under the third word because it is the word that I said.

- Look across the row at sample B. The key word is one. Take just one cookie. Which word is the word one . . . one? (the first word) The first word is one. Fill in the circle under the first word because it is the word that I said.

- Move your marker to the box with the number 1 and the balloon. The key word is shoe. Greta tied her shoe. Fill in the circle under the word shoe.

- Move your marker to the box with the number 2 and the bear. The key word is black. Where is the black paint? Fill in the circle under the word black.

- Move your marker to the box with the number 3 and the apple. The key word is stop. Before you cross the street, stop and look both ways. Fill in the circle under the word stop.

- Move your marker to the box with the number 4 and the grapes. The key word is now. Mother wants us to leave now. Fill in the circle under the word now.

- Move your marker to the box with the number 5 and the flag. The key word is were. They were going to have a picnic but it rained. Fill in the circle under the word were.

- Move your marker to the box with the number 6 and the key. The key word is alone. She felt all alone when her friends left. Fill in the circle under the word alone.

- Move your marker to the box with the number 7 and the cup and saucer. The key word is crown. The queen is wearing her crown. Fill in the circle under the word crown.

- Move your marker to the box with the number 8 and the schoolgirl, near the top of the second column. The key word is many. I have many cousins. Fill in the circle under the word many.

- Move your marker to the box with the number 9 and the books. The key word is present. She took a present to the party. Fill in the circle under the word present.

- Move your marker to the box with the number 10 and the schoolboy. The key word is off. He took off his coat. Fill in the circle under the word off.

- Move your marker to the box with the number 11 and the calculator. The key word is came. Jerry came to school with his brother. Fill in the circle under the word came.

- Move your marker to the box with the number 12 and the ladder. The key word is smile. She has a nice smile. Fill in the circle under the word smile.

- Move your marker to the box with the number 13 and the paintbrush. The key word is ran. George ran all the way home. Fill in the circle under the word ran.

- Move your marker to the box with the number 14 and the star. The key word is funny. The teacher told a funny story. Fill in the circle under the word funny.

Teacher Scripts

Reading Comprehension: Word Attack

SPP 69

- Turn to page _____ in your test booklet. Find the number _____ at the top of the page and put your finger on it. (Check to see if everyone has found the number.)

- On this page you will find some stories and pictures. You will choose a picture that matches the last word in each story. Put your marker under sample A at the top of the page. Read the story and look at the words below it. When you read the last word, you may not know it. The last word in this item starts with an h, just like hide and have. The pictures that go with the story show a shoe, a hoop, and a hat. The word shoe does not begin with an h. The word hoop begins with an h, but a hoop is not something a person would wear. The word hat begins with an h and is something that you wear. You should fill in the circle under the picture of a hat because the name of that picture is the same as the last word in the story.

- Now look across the top of the page at sample B. Read the story and look at the pictures below it. Which picture has a name that is the same as the last word in the story? (mouse) Mouse is the last word in the story. Fill in the circle under the picture of the mouse because the name of that picture is the same as the last word in the story.

- Now you will finish the page. Work by yourself. Read each story. Then find a picture under the story to match the last word in the story. Fill in the circle under your answer choice.

Reading Comprehension: Sentences (1 Sentence/3 Pictures)

SPP 70

- Turn to page _____ in your test booklet. Find the number _____ at the top of the page and put your finger on it. (Check to see if everyone has found the number.)

- On this page you will match pictures and sentences. Find the tree and the sample at the top of the page. Read the sentence. Now look at the three pictures. Look at each picture carefully and check it against the sentence. Find the picture that shows exactly what the whole sentence says. Which picture matches the whole sentence? (the third picture) Only the third picture shows a man feeding a dog. Which words in the sentence helped you find the correct picture? (man, dog) Why are the other pictures wrong? (The first picture shows a man feeding fish; the second picture shows a woman feeding a dog.) Fill in the answer circle under the third picture because it matches the whole sentence.

- Finish the rest of the page. Work by yourself. Remember to look for the picture that shows exactly what the sentence says. Fill in the circle under your answer choice.

Teacher Scripts

Reading Comprehension: Sentences (1 Picture/3 Sentences) | SPP 71 |

- Turn to page _____ in your test booklet. Find the number _____ at the top of the page and put your finger on it. (Check to see if everyone has found the number.)

- On this page you will match sentences to pictures. Look at the sample. There are a picture and three sentences. What does the picture show? (a boy bouncing a ball) Now read the sentences next to the picture. Which sentence tells what the picture shows? (The boy is bouncing the ball.) Yes, the third sentence matches the picture so fill in the answer circle next to the third sentence. Which words in the third sentence helped you match it to the picture? (boy, bouncing, ball) Why are the other answer choices wrong? (The first sentence says the boy is reading a book; the second says a girl can jump rope.)

- Finish the rest of the page. Work by yourself. Remember to look for the sentence that tells about the whole picture. Fill in the circle next to the sentence that best tells about the picture.

Reading Comprehension: Sentences (with Blanks) | SPP 72 |

- Turn to page _____ in your test booklet. Find the number _____ at the top of the page and put your finger on it. (Check to see if everyone has found the number.)

- On this page you will show how well you understand sentences. Look at the sample by the tree. Read the sentence with the blank. Find the word that fits best in the sentence. The second answer, track, is correct. The sentence should read: *The train is on the track.* Fill in the answer circle under the word track.

- Finish the rest of page. Work by yourself. Fill in the circle next to the word that best completes the sentence.

Reading Comprehension: Riddles | SPP 86 |

- Turn to page _____ in your test booklet. Find the number _____ at the top of the page and put your finger on it. (Check to see if everyone has found the number.)

- On this page you will solve some riddles. Put your marker on the sample at the top of the page. There are two sentences and three pictures in this sample. The pictures show a chair, a man, and a tree. Read the sentences to yourself while I read them aloud. I have legs. I am alive. Which picture has something to do with both sentences? (man) Yes, the picture of the man is correct because a man has legs and is alive. Fill in the circle under the man.

- Finish the rest of page. Work by yourself. Read each set of sentences. Then fill in the circle under your answer choice.

Teacher Scripts

Reading Comprehension: Stories

Note:

- The sample for *Reading Comprehension: Stories* consists of one page (page 73). A short story is followed by four questions. The skills tested in each story of this section are listed in the table of contents by page number. The skills tested in the sample include the following:

  Main Idea

  Details

  Reality and Fantasy

  Word Meanings

- The sample will familiarize the students with the story format.

- The Student Practice Pages for *Reading Comprehension: Stories* (pages 74–85) consist of four longer stories which are set up in groups of three pages each. One paragraph of a continued story appears on each page and is followed by four questions testing skills which are always in the same order.

Page 1	**Page 2**	**Page 3**
Cause/Effect	Main Idea	Drawing Conclusions
Identifying Feelings	Details	Inferring the Main Idea
Predicting Outcomes	Sequence	Reality and Fantasy
Word Meanings	Word Meanings	Word Meanings

- In this way, each story unit tests a full range of comprehension skills. If you include all four stories in your practice test, you will assess each skill four times, except for word meanings which will be assessed 12 times.

Reading Comprehension: Stories   SPP 73

- Turn to page _____ in your test booklet. Find the number _____ at the top of the page and put your finger on it. (Check to see if everyone has found the number.)

- On this page you will answer questions about the story you read. This whole page is a sample. Find the tree and read the story at the top of the page. Look at the four questions below it. Each question has four answer choices. Check back in the story to decide on your answers and then fill in the circles under your answer choices.

- Which answer did you choose for question number 1? (dinosaurs) This story is mainly about dinosaurs. Which answer did you choose for question number 2? (from their bones) Scientists learn about dinosaurs from their bones. Which answer did you choose for question number 3? (Yes) This story is about things that really happened. Which answer did you choose for question number 4? (meat eaters) Carnivores means meat eaters.

- Now you are ready to read more stories and answer questions about them.

Reading Comprehension: Stories 1–4   SPP 74–85

- Turn to page _____ in your test booklet. Find the number _____ at the top of the page and put your finger on it. (Check to see if everyone has found the number.)

- Work by yourself. Find the tree and read the story on the page. Answer the four questions. When you come to an arrow at the bottom of a page, turn to the next page. Keep going until you get to the stop sign.

Teacher Scripts

Spelling

Note:

- The formats for testing spelling skills differ widely among the tests, even from grade level to grade level. As often as possible, these testing formats are identified for you on the title line at the beginning of each script and practice page.

- You may want to give your students the benefit of trying all of these formats, or you may wish to use the spelling list on page 220 to create more practice pages of your own in the appropriate format(s).

Spelling Skills (CAT/CTBS)

| SPP 87 |

- Turn to page _____ in your test booklet. Find the number _____ at the top of the page and put your finger on it. (Check to see if everyone has found the number.)

- On this page you will find the correct spellings of the words that complete the sentences. Look at the samples at the top of the page. Find sample A. There is a sentence with a blank. The blank shows that a word is missing. Who will read the sentence? Now look at the four words under the sentence. One answer choice shows the right way to spell the word that is missing from the sentence. Which word shows the correct spelling? (the fourth word, b-i-r-d) Fill in the circle in front of the fourth word because it shows the correct spelling of the word bird.

- Now find sample B. Who will read the sentence? Now look at the four answer choices and find the correct spelling of the missing word. Which answer choice shows the correct spelling of the word that fits in the sentence? (the third word, w-a-t-c-h) Fill in the circle in front of the third word because it shows the correct spelling of the word watch.

- Work by yourself. Finish the rest of the page in the same way that we did the samples. Fill in the circle next to the word that is spelled correctly.

Spelling Skills (MAT/Book 2)

| SPP 88 |

- Turn to page _____ in your test booklet. Find the number _____ at the top of the page and put your finger on it. (Check to see if everyone has found the number.)

- On this page you will look for words that have spelling mistakes. Look at sample A. You will see a sentence with three words underlined. Read the sentence with the underlined words to yourself as I read it out loud. A loud noise scared the kitten. One of the words is spelled wrong. Which one is it? (pause) Yes, the second word, n-o-y-s-e, is misspelled. It should be spelled n-o-i-s-e. Fill in the answer circle under n-o-y-s-e because it is spelled wrong.

- Now do sample B by yourself. Read the sentence with the underlined words and find the one that is misspelled. (pause) Which underlined word has a spelling error? (the second one, c-h-i-l-d-e-r-n) Yes, it should be c-h-i-l-d-r-e-n. Fill in the answer circle under c-h-i-l-d-e-r-n because it is incorrect.

- Work by yourself. Finish the rest of the page in the same way that we did the samples. Fill in the circle under the word that is not spelled correctly.

Teacher Scripts

Spelling

Spelling (MAT/Book 1 and ITBS/Book A)

SPP 89

- Turn to page _____ in your test booklet. Find the number _____ at the top of the page and put your finger on it. (Check to see if everyone has found the number.)

- On this page you will look for words that have spelling mistakes. Look at sample A. Look at the three words and listen to this sentence: Do you now (know) how to jump rope? One of the words is spelled wrong. Which one is it? Is it now, jump, or rope? (pause) Yes, the first word, n-o-w, is misspelled. It should be spelled k-n-o-w. Fill in the first answer circle.

- Now do sample B by yourself. Look at the three words and listen to this sentence: I gave the candie (candy) to your mother. One of the words is spelled wrong. Is it gave, candie, or mother? (pause) Yes, the second word, c-a-n-d-i-e, is misspelled. It should be spelled c-a-n-d-y. Fill in the second answer circle.

- Now you will do more items like the samples. Listen to each sentence while you look at the words. Fill in the circle in front of the word that is misspelled.

- Move down to number 1. Listen to this sentence: He drank a large glass of watter (water). Which word is spelled wrong? Is it large, glass, or watter? Fill in the circle next to your answer choice.

- Move down to number 2. Listen to this sentence: Please wait untill (until) I finish. Which word is spelled wrong? Is it please, untill, or finish? Fill in the circle next to your answer choice.

- Move down to number 3. Listen to this sentence: Jeff walks to skool (school) every day. Which word is spelled wrong? Is it walks, skool, or every? Fill in the circle next to your answer choice.

- Move down to number 4. Listen to this sentence: Her famly (family) is going to move soon. Which word is spelled wrong? Is it famly, going, or move? Fill in the circle next to your answer choice.

- Move down to number 5. Listen to this sentence: We are going to eat lunch at nune (noon). Which word is spelled wrong? Is it going, lunch, or nune? Fill in the circle next to your answer choice.

- Move up to number 6 in the second column. Listen to this sentence: It was a cold and windy nite (night). Which word is spelled wrong? Is it cold, windy, or nite? Fill in the circle next to your answer choice.

- Move down to number 7. Listen to this sentence: Where did you putt (put) the money? Which word is spelled wrong? Is it where, putt, or money? Fill in the circle next to your answer choice.

- Move down to number 8. Listen to this sentence: The polar bear was very wite (white). Which word is spelled wrong? Is it polar, bear, or wite? Fill in the circle next to your answer choice.

- Move down to number 9. Listen to this sentence: The leavs (leaves) on the trees were brown. Which word is spelled wrong? Is it leavs, trees, or brown? Fill in the circle next to your answer choice.

- Move down to number 10. Listen to this sentence: You can always trie (try) again. Which word is spelled wrong? Is it always, trie, or again? Fill in the circle next to your answer choice.

Teacher Scripts

Spelling

Spelling (MAT/Book A, SAT/Book A, and TAAS)

- Turn to page _____ in your test booklet. Find the number _____ at the top of the page and put your finger on it. (Check to see if everyone has found the number.)

- On this page you will show what words you know how to spell. Look at sample A. There are four words with answer spaces beside them in the sample. I am going to say a word, then read a sentence using the word, and then say the word one more time. Listen and look at the answer choices. Make . . . I know how to make cookies . . . make. Which answer choice shows the right spelling of the word make? (the last one) The last word, m-a-k-e, gives the right spelling of make. Fill in the circle beside the last word.

- Now look at sample B. Listen and find the right spelling of the word I say. Pet . . . I have a pet turtle . . . pet. Which answer choice shows the right spelling of pet? (the first one) Fill in the circle beside the first word because it is spelled correctly.

- Now we will do the rest of the page. I will read the word for each question and the sentence that goes with it. Listen and fill in the circle beside the right spelling of the word.

- Find item number 1. wall . . . They are building a wall . . . wall.

- Move down to item 2. wish . . . Did you wish on that star? . . . wish.

- Move down to item 3. stop . . . They forgot to stop for the red light . . . stop.

- Move down to item 4. maybe . . . Maybe we will go to the zoo this weekend . . . maybe.

- Move down to item 5. lamb . . . Mary had a little lamb . . . lamb.

- Find item 6 near the top of the right-hand column. keep . . . His mother let him keep the kitten . . . keep.

- Move down to item 7. ranch . . . My uncle has a ranch with lots of horses . . . ranch.

- Move down to item 8. game . . . I watched the football game on TV with my father . . . game.

- Move down to item 9. walking . . . I saw her when I was walking to school . . . walking.

- Move down to item 10. very . . . It is very stormy outside today . . . very.

Spelling (SAT/Book A)

- Turn to page _____ in your test booklet. Find the number _____ at the top of the page and put your finger on it. (Check to see if everyone has found the number.)

- On this page you will find words that are not spelled correctly. Look at the sample A. There are four words in this sample: animals . . . barn . . . balloon . . . curly. Find the word that is not spelled correctly. (b-a-l-o-o-n) Fill in the circle in front of the third word. The word is balloon, and it should be spelled b-a-l-l-o-o-n.

- Look at sample B. The four words are children . . . desk . . . chair . . . teacher. Which word is not spelled correctly? (c-h-i-l-d-e-r-n) The word is children, and it should be spelled c-h-i-l-d-r-e-n. Fill in the circle before the first word because it is spelled wrong.

- Finish the rest of this page on your own. In each item, fill in the answer circle in front of the word that is misspelled.

Teacher Scripts

Spelling

Spelling Skills (ITBS/Book 2)

- Turn to page _____ in your test booklet. Find the number _____ at the top of the page and put your finger on it. (Check to see if everyone has found the number.)

- On this page you will find words that are misspelled. I will say three words that are printed in your book, and then I will use them in a sentence. You will find the word that is misspelled.

- Look at the words in sample A. They are mother, visit, and month. Listen carefully: My mother will visit my grandparents next month. Which word is spelled wrong? (munth) Fill in the circle under the last answer choice m-u-n-t-h because it is a misspelling of m-o-n-t-h.

- Look at sample B. The three words are best, subject, and math. Listen carefully: My best subject in school is math. Which of the words is spelled wrong? (suject) Fill in the circle under the second answer choice, s-u-j-e-c-t, because it is a misspelling of s-u-b-j-e-c-t.

- Now we will do the rest of the page in the same way that we did the samples. Look at the words and listen to what I say. Fill in the circle under the word that is spelled wrong.

- Move down to number 1. watch, game, night: Did you watch the game on television last night? Fill in the circle by your answer choice.

- Move down to number 2. they, lunch, o'clock: They will eat lunch at twelve o'clock. Fill in the circle by your answer choice.

- Move down to number 3. large, airplane, house: A large airplane flew over our house. Fill in the circle by your answer choice.

- Move down to number 4. bottom, fell, sack: The bottom fell out of his lunch sack. Fill in the circle by your answer choice.

- Find number 5 near the top of the right hand column. truck, parked, street: A truck was parked on our street. Fill in the circle by your answer choice.

- Move down to number 6. study, together, school: Let's study together after school. Fill in the circle by your answer choice.

- Move down to number 7. wanted, trade, cookies: He wanted to trade cookies at lunch. Fill in the circle by your answer choice.

- Move down to number 8. mother, baking, dinner: My mother is baking a chicken for dinner. Fill in the circle by your answer choice.

Teacher Scripts

Language Mechanics: Capitalization (CAT/CTBS/MAT/TAAS) | SPP 93

- Turn to page _____ in your test booklet. Find the number _____ at the top of the page and put your finger on it. (Check to see if everyone has found the number.)
- On this page you will find words that should begin with capital letters. Look at the samples at the top of the page. Find sample A. The sentence is divided into three parts. Look at each part of the sentence. Is there a part of the sentence that needs a capital letter? (yes, the first part) Why? (The name of a month always begins with a capital letter.) Fill in the answer circle under the first part of the sentence because it needs a capital letter.
- Look at sample B. What is the word that comes after the sentence. (none) You will fill in the answer circle under the word none only if no more capital letters are needed in a sentence. Now read the sentence in sample B. Is there a word in any of the three parts of the sentence that needs a capital letter? (no) Fill in the circle under the word none.
- Finish the rest of this page by yourself in the same way that we did the samples. Read each sentence. Look for the part that needs a capital letter. If no capital letters are missing, fill in the circle under the word none.

Language Mechanics: Capitalization (SAT) | SPP 94

- Turn to page _____ in your test booklet. Find the number _____ at the top of the page and put your finger on it. (Check to see if everyone has found the number.)
- On this page you will listen to a sentence being read aloud and choose the correct capitalization for the sentence. Find sample A and put your marker underneath the tree. There are three words in this sample: airplanes . . . very . . . noisy. You will hear these words in the sentence I am about to read. Listen closely: Airplanes are very noisy. Which word should start with a capital letter: airplanes, very, or noisy? (airplanes) Yes, the correct answer is airplanes because it should begin with a capital letter. Fill in the answer circle by the word airplanes.
- Look at sample B and the piggy bank. Listen to this sentence: She asked Mary to water the plants. Which word should start with a capital letter: asked, Mary, or water? Here is the sentence again: She asked Mary to water the plants. Which word should be capitalized? (Mary) Yes, the correct answer is Mary because it is a person's name, and it should begin with a capital letter. Fill in the answer circle by the word Mary.
- Move your marker to the balloon. Listen to this sentence: My father and I like to play ball. Which word should begin with a capital letter: I, like, or ball? Here is the sentence again: My father and I like to play ball.
- Move your marker to the bear. Listen to this sentence: The basketball game will be on Tuesday evening. Which word should begin with a capital letter: basketball, Tuesday, or evening? Here is the sentence again: The basketball game will be on Tuesday evening.
- Move your marker to the grapes. Listen to this sentence: When will the party start? Which word should begin with a capital letter: when, party, or start? Here is the sentence again: "When will the party start?"
- Move your marker to the schoolgirl. Listen to this sentence: My birthday card was from Uncle David. Which word should begin with a capital letter: birthday, card, or uncle? Here is the sentence again: My birthday card was from Uncle David.
- Move your marker to the books. Listen to this sentence: They went whitewater rafting on the Truckee River. Which word should begin with a capital letter: whitewater, rafting, or river? Here is the sentence again: They went whitewater rafting on the Truckee River.
- Move your marker to the schoolboy. Listen to this sentence: Is Miss Lauder your homeroom teacher? Which word should begin with a capital letter: miss, homeroom, or teacher? Here is the sentence again: Is Miss Lauder your homeroom teacher?

Teacher Scripts

Language Mechanics: Capitalization (ITBS) SPP 95

- Turn to page _____ in your test booklet. Find the number _____ at the top of the page and put your finger on it. (Check to see if everyone has found the number.)

- On this page you will look for capitalization mistakes in sentences. Look at sample A. It is a story which has been divided into three parts. One part of the story has a capitalization mistake in it. Read the story to yourself while I read it out loud.

> My mother and I went
>
> shopping yesterday. today
>
> she will take my sister.

- Which part needs another capital letter? (the second line) The second line has a mistake in it because today should begin with a capital letter since it is the first word in a sentence. Fill in the circle beside the second line.

- Find sample B. Read the story to yourself while I read it out loud.

> Many people vacation in
>
> California. They like to go
>
> to disneyland.

- Which part needs another capital letter? (the third line) The third line has a mistake because Disneyland should begin with a capital letter since it is the name of a particular place. Fill in the circle beside the third line.

- Now we will do the rest of the page. Read the items to yourself while I read them out loud. On each item, fill in the answer circle in front of the part that is missing a capital letter.

- Number 1: It snowed in Hawaii last week. They seldom get snow, even in february.

- Number 2: Jimmy and i went to the movies last night. We had great popcorn.

- Number 3: Our school is named after President Lincoln. It is on main Street near the park.

- Number 4: My favorite basketball team is the Los Angeles lakers. Who is your favorite team?

- Number 5: Kelly's birthday is on Saint Patrick's Day. She is irish.

- Number 6: My little sister likes to watch barney. He used to be my favorite too.

Teacher Scripts

Language Mechanics: Capitalization (ITBS) *cont.*

- Number 7:   A woman named mrs. Brown just moved in next door. We made some cookies for her.
- Number 8:   What is the name of your favorite book? Mine is called *matilda* by Roald Dahl.

Language Mechanics: Capitalization (ITBS)

- Turn to page _____ in your test booklet. Find the number _____ at the top of the page and put your finger on it. (Check to see if everyone has found the number.)

- On this page you will find words that should begin with capital letters. Look at samples A and B. In these samples, there is a sentence written above two lines. Read the first line of the sentence. Do you see a word that needs a capital letter? (yes) Which word is it? (his) Why should his begin with a capital letter? (The first word of a sentence always begins with a capital letter.) Read the second line of the sentence. Do you see a word that needs a capital letter? (june) Why should june begin with a capital letter? (The name of a month always begins with a capital letter.) Now, let me show you how to mark your answers. The words in the sentence sit above answer circles. Fill in the circle under the first letter of his because his should begin with a capital letter. Then fill in the circle under the first letter of june because june also needs a capital letter.

- Look at the sentence again. The word sister's also has a circle under it, but you should not fill it in because sister's does not need a capital in this sentence.

- Now look at samples C and D. Read the first line of the sentence to yourself and look at the words with circles under the first letters. Do you see any words that should begin with capital letters? (yes) Which words? (*little women*) Why do these words need capital letters? (The important words in the title of a book always begin with capital letters.) Fill in the circles under *little* and *women*. Now read the second line of the sentence. Should the word with a circle under it begin with a capital letter? (no) If a word with a circle under it does not need a capital letter, do not fill in the circle.

- Do the rest of the page in the same way that we did the samples. Work by yourself. Remember to look for words that need capital letters.

Teacher Scripts

Language Mechanics: Punctuation (CAT/CTBS)
SPP 97

- Turn to page _____ in your test booklet. Find the number _____ at the top of the page and put your finger on it. (Check to see if everyone has found the number.)

- On this page you will look for places where punctuation marks are needed in sentences. Look at sample A. Put your marker on the tree. Read the sentence. Now look at the four punctuation marks underneath the sentence. What are they? (period, comma, question mark, and exclamation point) Is one of these punctuation marks needed in the sentence? (yes) Which one? (the period) Yes, the sentence is a telling sentence, and a period is always used at the end of a telling sentence. Fill in the answer circle in front of the period to show that it is needed in the sentence. Now look at the word at the end of the row of punctuation marks. What is it? (none) You will need to fill in the circle in front of the word none only if the sentence does not need any more punctuation marks.

- Now look at sample B. Put your marker on the piggy bank. Read the sentence to yourself and then fill in the circle for the punctuation mark that is needed in the sentence. Fill in the circle for none if the punctuation is already correct. Which answer circle did you fill in? (the fifth one, none) Why? (The sentence is correct; no more punctuation marks are needed in the sentence.)

- Do the rest of the page in the same way that we did the samples. Work by yourself. Remember to look for a punctuation mark that might be needed in each sentence.

Language Mechanics: Punctuation (ITBS)
SPP 98

- Turn to page _____ in your test booklet. Find the number _____ at the top of the page and put your finger on it. (Check to see if everyone has found the number.)

- On this page you will look for punctuation mistakes in sentences. Look at sample A. It is a story divided into three parts. One part of the story needs a punctuation mark. Read the story to yourself while I read it out loud.

  My friend's cat had kittens
  last week. I hope that I will get
  to have one of them

- Which part needs a punctuation mark? (the third part) The third part has a mistake because the sentence should end with a period. Fill in the circle beside the third line.

- Find sample B. Read the story to yourself while I read it out loud.

  Stop The traffic is very
  heavy here. Let's wait for a
  new green light.

- Which part needs another punctuation mark? (the first part) The first part has a mistake because Stop should be followed by an exclamation point. Fill in the circle beside the first line.

- Now we will do the rest of the page. Read the items to yourself while I read them out loud. Fill in the circle in front of the part that needs another punctuation mark.

Teacher Scripts

Language Mechanics: Punctuation (ITBS) *cont.*

- Number 1: Mr. Whitehead said to us,
  The museum is over there.
  We had finally arrived.

- Number 2: Next month we will have a
  party for our parents. They
  were married May 21 1985.

- Number 3: My name is G L Cramer. I
  like to be called by my initials.
  It makes me feel special.

- Number 4: Has anyone seen my baseball
  mitt I thought I left it on the
  kitchen table.

- Number 5: It is too noisy in here,
  said Tran. The movie theater
  was having a kids' matinee.

- Number 6: We picked up all of our
  toys and put them away. Mom
  said it looked much neater

- Number 7: Where are you going If you
  are going to the store, may I go
  with you?

- Number 8: Help Please get the teacher.
  Jill fell off a swing and
  hurt herself.

Teacher Scripts

Language Mechanics: Punctuation (ITBS)

- Turn to page _____ in your test booklet. Find the number _____ at the top of the page and put your finger on it. (Check to see if everyone has found the number.)

- On this page you will look for places where punctuation marks are needed. Look at samples A and B. It says **Question Marks** above the sentence. The sentence is written over two lines. Read the first line of the sentence. Is a question mark needed in this line? (no) Read the second line. Do you see a place where a question mark is needed? (yes) Where? (at the end of the sentence) Yes, the sentence asks a question, and a question mark is always used at the end of an asking sentence, or question. Now, let's find the answers. They are the places in the sentence with circles underneath them. Fill in the circle at the end of the sentence because that is where a question mark is needed.

- Look at the sentence again. Where else do you see answer circles? (below Mr and leader) Is a punctuation mark needed after Mr? (yes, a period) That's right, but in this sentence you are only looking for a place where question marks are needed, so you should not fill in the circle below Mr. Is a punctuation mark needed after leader? (no) A punctuation mark is not needed after leader, so you should not fill in the circle below leader.

- Now look at samples C and D. It says **Commas** above the sentence. Read the sentence to yourself and fill in the circles under any places where commas are needed. Do not fill in circles where any other punctuation mark is needed or where a punctuation mark is not needed at all. Did you find any places where commas are needed? (yes) Where? (after Jacksonville) That's right. A comma is needed after the name of a city when it is followed by the name of a state.

- Now we are ready to do the rest of the page in the same way that we did the samples. You will work by yourself on one part of the lesson at a time. Look at the box on the left that says **Question Marks** at the top. Read the story in the box and fill in the circles under all of the places where question marks are needed. Stop when you finish the story.

- Look at the next box. It says **Periods** at the top. Read the story in the box and fill in the circles under all of the places where periods are needed. Stop when you finish the story.

- Look at the next box. It says **Quotation Marks** at the top. Read the story in the box and fill in the circles under all of the places where quotation marks are needed. Stop when you finish the story.

- Find the box near the top of the second column that says **Commas** at the top. Read the story in the box and fill in the circles under all of the places where commas are needed. Stop when you finish the story.

- Look at the next box. It says **Apostrophes** at the top. Read the story in the box and fill in the circles under all of the places where apostrophes are needed. Stop when you finish the story.

- Look at the next box. It says **Exclamation Points** at the top. Read the story in the box and fill in the circles under all of the places where exclamation points are needed. Stop when you finish the story.

Teacher Scripts

Language Mechanics: Punctuation (MAT/SAT/TAAS)

- Turn to page _____ in your test booklet. Find the number _____ at the top of the page and put your finger on it. (Check to see if everyone has found the number.)
- On this page you will choose a word and a punctuation mark to complete each sentence. Look at sample A. Read the sentence to yourself as I read it out loud. The giraffe ate leaves . . . The giraffe ate leaves. Does the sentence ask something or tell something? (tells something) What mark belongs at the end of a sentence that tells something? (a period) Now look at the punctuation marks after the word leaves. Where should you fill in your answer? (beside the answer choice that has a period)
- Look at sample B. Read the sentence to yourself as I read it out loud. Then find the punctuation mark that belongs at the end of the sentence. Listen: Did you find your book? . . . Did you find your book? Which mark is needed? (a question mark) Why? (The sentence asks something.) Fill in the circle beside the word book followed by a question mark because a sentence that asks something always ends in a question mark.
- Now we will do the rest of the page. I will read each sentence two times. You should fill in the circle beside the answer that shows the correct punctuation for the sentence.
- Move down to number 1 under the samples: Mary went to practice . . . Mary went to practice.
- Move down to number 2: Aren't they going to come? . . . Aren't they going to come?
- Move down to number 3: Can you play this afternoon? . . . Can you play this afternoon?
- Move down to number 4: His birthday is tomorrow . . . His birthday is tomorrow.
- Move up to number 5 near the top of the right column: Stop hurting me! . . . Stop hurting me!
- Move down to number 6: Who can do the problem? . . . Who can do the problem?
- Move down to number 7: Where are you going? . . . Where are you going?
- Move down to number 8: The book is on the table . . . The book is on the table.

Language Mechanics: Capitalization and Punctuation

Note:

- The formats for testing these skills differ widely among the tests but, in general, fall into two categories: identifying correctly capitalized and punctuated sentences and proofreading passages with errors. These two categories are covered on pages 101 and 102.

Language Mechanics: Capitalization and Punctuation
(Identifying Correct Sentences)

- Turn to page _____ in your test booklet. Find the number _____ at the top of the page and put your finger on it. (Check to see if everyone has found the number.)
- On this page you will look for correct capitalization and punctuation. Look at sample A. Read the sentences. Only one of these sentences is written correctly. Which sentence is written correctly with no capitalization or punctuation mistakes? (the last one) Yes, the last sentence has no mistakes. Fill in the circle in front of the last sentence.
- Now look at sample B. Read the sentences to yourself. Then fill in the circle in front of the sentence that does not have any mistakes in it. Which one did you mark? (the first one) You should have marked the circle in front of the first sentence because it is the only one without mistakes in it.
- Work by yourself to finish the page. Remember to look for the sentence in each section that does not have any capitalization or punctuation mistakes in it.

Teacher Scripts

Language Mechanics: Capitalization and Punctuation
(Proofing for Errors)

- Turn to page _____ in your test booklet. Find the number _____ at the top of the page and put your finger on it. (Check to see if everyone has found the number.)

- On this page you will look for correct capitalization and punctuation in a letter. Look at the letter in the sample. It is in the box on the left. Read the letter. Now look at the underlined words in the letter. The capital letter A under these words tells you that this part of the letter is Item A. What words are underlined? (Aspen colorado) Aspen is the name of a city, and Colorado is the name of a state. Should these words begin with capital letters? (yes) Look at the underlined words again. Is the capitalization of these words correct? (no) What is wrong? (Colorado should be capitalized.) Should a punctuation mark be used between the names of a city and a state when they are written together? (yes) What mark should be used? (a comma) Is the punctuation of the underlined words correct? (no) What is wrong? (a comma is missing) Now look at the answer choices next to the letter. Check them carefully and find the one that shows the words Aspen and Colorado beginning with capital letters with a comma between the words. Which answer did you choose? (the third one) Fill in the circle in front of the third answer choice because it shows the correct capitalization and punctuation for the underlined part of the letter.

- Look at the answer choices again. Read the last answer choice. (correct as it is) You should fill in this answer space if the underlined part of the letter already has the correct capitalization and punctuation.

- Work by yourself to finish the page. Read the letter and do items 1 through 4 in the same way that we did the sample. The underlined parts of the letter have numbers under them. To find the answer choices, match the number under each underlined part to the same number in front of the answer choices below. Carefully check all of the answer choices for each item. Then fill in the circle in front of the answer that shows the correct capitalization and punctuation.

Teacher Scripts

Language Expression: Usage (Sentences) `SPP 103`

- Turn to page _____ in your test booklet. Find the number _____ at the top of the page and put your finger on it. (Check to see if everyone has found the number.)

- On this page you will choose the best words to complete the sentences. Look at sample A. Find the sentence with a blank. The blank means that one or more words are missing. Read the sentence. Now read the two words under the sentence. What are they? (has, have) Let's read the sentence again, but this time let's put each of these answer choices in place of the blank. Only one of the answer choices is right. Which word fits best in the sentence? (have) What is the complete sentence? (Our friends have a new car.) Fill in the circle in front of the word have because have is the best word to complete the sentence.

- Look at sample B. This item has four answer choices instead of two. Read the sentence. Now look at the four words under the sentence. Read the sentence to yourself with each of the answer choices in the blank. Which word fits best in the sentence? (low) What is the complete sentence? (That airplane is flying too low.) Fill in the circle in front of the word low.

- Work by yourself to finish the page in the same way that we did the samples. Some of the questions will have two answer choices, and some will have four. Be sure to look at all of the answer choices before deciding on an answer. Stop at the end of the page.

Language Expression: Usage (Passages) `SPP 104`

- Turn to page _____ in your test booklet. Find the number _____ at the top of the page and put your finger on it. (Check to see if everyone has found the number.)

- On this page you will find the best word or words to complete a story. Look at sample A. Look at the directions at the top of the page. Read them to yourself as I read them aloud: Read the story. Decide which word or group of words fits best in each blank.

- Let's look at the sample story. It has blanks that show where a word or a group of words is missing. One answer choice fits best in each blank. Read the story and answer choices for sample A. Which answer choice fits best in the blank? (started) The third answer, started, is correct. Fill in the answer circle beside the word started.

- Now do sample B by yourself. Read the story and decide which answer fits in blank B. Which answer is correct? The second answer choice, thought, fits best in the blank. Fill in the circle beside thought.

- Work by yourself to finish the page. Read the stories and then fill in the circle beside the answer that fits in each blank in the story. Remember, the answer choices for a blank should be labeled with the same number as the blank.

Teacher Scripts

Language Expression: Pronouns

SPP 105

- Turn to page _____ in your test booklet. Find the number _____ at the top of the page and put your finger on it. (Check to see if everyone has found the number.)

- On this page you will choose words that can take the place of other words. Look at sample A. Read the sentence. What are the underlined words? (Mary and Fred) Now read the answer choices. Which answer choice is a word that could take the place of the underlined words? (They) The word They is the correct answer. Instead of saying Mary and Fred are at the park, the sentence could say They are at the park. Fill in the answer circle in front of the word They.

- Let's look at sample B. Read the sentence and look at the underlined words. Now read the four answer choices. Fill in the answer circle that has a word that can take the place of the underlined words. Which answer circle did you fill in? (the third one) That's right. Instead of saying Please put the ball in the box, you could say Please put it in the box. The word it can take the place of the words the ball.

- Work by yourself to finish this page. Read the sentences and the answer choices. Choose the answer choice that can take the place of the underlined word(s) in each sentence.

Language Expression: Sentences

> **Note:** The formats for testing this skill differ widely among the tests but, in general, fall into four categories: subject and predicate, correct word order, kind of sentence, and complete sentence. These categories are covered on pages 106–109.

Language Expression: Sentences
(Subjects and Predicates: CAT/CTBS)

SPP 106

- Turn to page _____ in your test booklet. Find the number _____ at the top of the page and put your finger on it. (Check to see if everyone has found the number.)

- On this page you will choose the best words to complete the sentences. Look at sample A. The sentence has a blank line in it. The blank shows that part of the sentence is missing. Read the sentence. Remember to say the word blank when you come to the line. Read the three answers under the sentence. Find the answer that sounds right and makes sense with the other words in the sentence. Read the sentence to yourself with the first answer in place of the blank. Next try the second answer in place of the blank. Then try the last answer. Read carefully. Which answer best completes the sentence? (the second answer, are funny) Look at the answers again. Fill in the circle in front of the words are funny because are funny is the answer that best completes the sentence.

- Look across the page to sample B. Read the sentence to yourself. Say the word blank when you come to the line in the sentence. Then read the three answers under the sentence in place of the blank. Doing this will help you find the one that best completes the sentence. Which answer sounds right and makes sense in the sentence? (the last answer, The school bus) What is the complete sentence? (The school bus is full.) Fill in the circle in front of the words The school bus, because The school bus is the answer that best completes the sentence.

- Now work by yourself to finish the page. Read each sentence. Then read the words under the sentence. Fill in the circle in front of the words that best complete the sentence.

Teacher Scripts

Language Expression: Sentences — SPP 107
(Word Order: CAT/CTBS/MAT)

- Turn to page _____ in your test booklet. Find the number _____ at the top of the page and put your finger on it. (Check to see if everyone has found the number.)

- On this page you will find questions that have been made from the words in sentences. Look at the samples. Find sample A. Read the sentence. Under the sentence are three questions. All three questions are made from the words in the sentence, but only one of the questions has the words in an order that makes sense. Read the questions to yourself now. Which question has the words in the right order? (the second question) What is the correct question? (Is Mother coming now?) Fill in the circle in front of the second question because it has the words in the right order for a question.

- Look across the page to sample B. Read the sentence. Read the three questions. Which question has the words from the sentence in the right order? (the first one) Yes, that is correct because all of the words from the sentence are in the right order. Fill in the circle in front of the first question.

- Now work by yourself to finish the page. Read each item carefully. Then fill in the circle in front of the question that has the words in the right order.

Language Expression: Sentences — SPP 108
(Kind of Sentence: MAT)

- Turn to page _____ in your test booklet. Find the number _____ at the top of the page and put your finger on it. (Check to see if everyone has found the number.)

- On this page you will decide if groups of words make up sentences. Look at the group of words in the sample at the top of the page. Read it to yourself as I read it out loud. They ran fast. Do the words make a complete sentence? (yes) Does the sentence ask something or tell something? (it tells something) They ran fast is a complete sentence that tells something. You have three answer choices on this page—Telling, Asking, and No Sentence. Which answer circle should you fill? (under the word Telling)

- Now we are ready to do the rest of this page. I will read each group of words two times. You need to decide what kind of sentence each group of words makes and then fill in the circle for your answer. If the words do not make a complete sentence, fill in the circle underneath No Sentence. Listen carefully.

- Find number 1: Martin wants some milk . . . Martin wants some milk

- Move down to number 2: Have you ever visited the zoo . . . Have you ever visited the zoo

- Move down to number 3: Going to the grocery store . . . Going to the grocery store

- Move down to number 4: Does he plan to watch the game . . . Does he plan to watch the game

- Move down to number 5: To the park by my house . . . To the park by my house

- Move down to number 6: I returned the book yesterday . . . I returned the book yesterday

Teacher Scripts

Language Expression: Sentences SPP 109
(Complete Sentences: SAT)

- Turn to page _____ in your test booklet. Find the number _____ at the top of the page and put your finger on it. (Check to see if everyone has found the number.)
- On this page you will decide which groups of words are complete sentences. Look at each group of words in sample A as I read them to you. With a blue balloon . . . José waited for his turn . . . Passed him the ball. Which group of words is a complete sentence? (the second one) Yes, the second group of words is a complete sentence: José waited for his turn. Fill in the circle before the second group of words.
- Now look at each group of words in sample B as I read them to you. The store by the park . . . Through wind and rain . . . Maria plays the piano. Which group of words is a complete sentence? (the third one) Yes, the third group of words is a complete sentence: Maria plays the piano. Fill in the circle before the third group of words.
- Now we will do the rest of the page. Listen carefully as I read each group of words.
- Put your marker to item 1 at the top of the first column under the samples. Which one of these is a complete sentence? Those are rain clouds . . . Pink clouds in the west . . . Looking out the window.
- Move your marker to item 2. Which one of these is a complete sentence? The dog loves her puppies . . . Eating the dog food . . . Spotted white and black.
- Move your marker down under item 3. Which one of these is a complete sentence? Ten candles on the cake . . . Pink frosting and roses . . . Today is my birthday.
- Move your marker to item 4. Which one of these is a complete sentence? We walked home from school . . . Carrying lots of paintings . . . Many good television shows.
- Move your marker to item 5. Which one of these is a complete sentence? Two chocolate chip cookies . . . I'm hungry for my lunch . . . Standing in a long line.
- Move your marker up to item 6, near the top of the second column. Which one of these is a complete sentence? With two overdue books . . . Maria goes to the library . . . Reading a good book.
- Move your marker to item 7. Which one of these is a complete sentence? Holding my report card . . . With excellent grades . . . Mother will be happy.
- Move your marker to item 8. Which one of these is a complete sentence? Under the garden gate . . . My dog, Arfie, ran away . . . Before it gets really dark.
- Move your marker to item 9. Which one of these is a complete sentence? Jumped rope really fast . . . Lots of hard homework . . . Where is your lunchbox?
- Move your marker to item 10. Which one of these is a complete sentence? Always makes pancakes . . . My brother feels happy . . . Upstairs in my bedroom.

Language Expression: Sentences SPP 110
(Proofing Passages: TAAS)

- Turn to page _____ in your test booklet. Find the number _____ at the top of the page and put your finger on it. (Check to see if everyone has found the number.)
- On this page you will decide if the sentences in a story are correct. Let's read the directions at the top of the page. (Read the directions to the students.)
- Now read the story in sample A. One sentence in the story is underlined. Decide which answer choice is the correct way to write the underlined part in the story. If the underlined part is correct, choose no mistake.
- Which answer choice is the correct way to write the underlined part in the story? (the second answer choice) Fill in the circle beside the second answer.
- Now work by yourself to finish this page. Read each story. Fill in the circle beside the answer choice that is the correct way to write the underlined part in the story. If the underlined part is correct, choose no mistake.

Teacher Scripts

Language Expression: Sentence Sequence

- Turn to page _____ in your test booklet. Find the number _____ at the top of the page and put your finger on it. (Check to see if everyone has found the number.)

- On this page you will put the sentences of paragraphs in order. Look at sample A. Each sentence has a number in front of it. Read sentence 1. Read sentence 2. Read sentence 3. The three sentences make a paragraph, but the sentences are not in the right order. Some of the sentences have key words that will help you figure out the right order. Find the word *Next* in sentence 3. A sentence that begins with the word *Next* is usually not the first sentence in a paragraph. Find the word *Finally* in sentence 2. A sentence that begins with the word *Finally* usually comes near the end of a paragraph. Now read the sentences again. Which sentence should come first in the paragraph? (sentence 1) Which sentence should come second? (sentence 3) Read the paragraph with the sentences in the right order.

- Now look at the answer choices under the sentences. They show the numbers 1, 2, and 3 in different orders. The number 1 stands for sentence 1, the number 2 stands for sentence 2, and the number 3 for sentence 3. If the correct order for the sentences is sentence 1, sentence 3, sentence 2, which answer choice is correct? (the second one) Fill in the circle next to the second choice because it shows 1-3-2 for the correct order of the sentences.

- Look at sample B. Read the three sentences to yourself and look for key words that will help you figure out the order of the sentences. Did you find any key words? (*Then* in sentence 2) A sentence that begins with the word *Then* is usually not the first sentence in a paragraph. Now read the sentences again and figure out the order in which things happened. What is the correct order for the sentences in paragraph B? (sentence 3, sentence 1, sentence 2) Read the paragraph with the sentences in the correct order. Now look at the answer choices. Which answer choice shows the numbers in the correct order for the sentences in the paragraph? (the last one) Fill in the circle in front of the last answer choice.

- Work by yourself to finish this page. Read each set of sentences carefully and look for key words that will help you figure out the order in which things happened. Fill in the circle next to the choice that shows the correct order of the sentences.

Language Expression: Paragraphs

- Turn to page _____ in your test booklet. Find the number _____ at the top of the page and put your finger on it. (Check to see if everyone has found the number.)

- On this page you will read parts of paragraphs and choose the sentences that will complete them. Look at the sample. Read the story with the blank to yourself. Under the story are four sentences. One of these sentences fits in the blank space in the story. Which sentence should go in the blank? (the second one) Yes, the second sentence matches the content of the rest of the story. Fill in the answer circle in front of the second sentence.

- Do the rest of the stories by yourself just as we did the samples. Read each answer choice and pick the one that matches the content of the rest of the paragraph. Fill in the circle in front of your answer.

Teacher Scripts

Language Expression: Writing

Note:

- The TAAS test includes three student-generated writing samples: descriptive, informative, and narrative. Each one includes a page of instructions and guidelines to help the students get organized. The teacher reads these aloud while the students read along. Students are encouraged to use scratch paper to brainstorm and make notes. The prompts for the descriptive and narrative writing pieces are pictures.
- The tests include instructions and time for pre-writing and writing a first draft. Writing samples are scored with a rubric. If you use the writing process, both you and your students will be familiar with this procedure.
- The scoring emphasis is on content. The only time for concern about errors in mechanics is when there are so many of them that it is hard to read the piece.

Language Expression: Descriptive Writing (TAAS) SPP 113

- Turn to page _____ in your test booklet. Find the number _____ at the top of the page and put your finger on it. (Check to see if everyone has found the number.)
- In this lesson you will write about a picture. Before you begin writing, you will use scratch paper to brainstorm and organize your ideas.
- Use the best English you can but do not worry about mistakes. The most important thing is to write clearly about the picture and tell about all of the things you see in the picture. Use the notes that you made on the scratch paper to stay organized.

Language Expression: Informative Writing (TAAS) SPP 114

- Turn to page _____ in your test booklet. Find the number _____ at the top of the page and put your finger on it. (Check to see if everyone has found the number.)
- In this lesson you will write about how to do something. Before you begin writing, you will use scratch paper to list all of the steps you should take and then organize them in order from first to last.
- Use the best English you can but do not worry about mistakes. The most important thing is to describe every step in the correct order. Use the notes that you made on the scratch paper to stay organized.

Language Expression: Narrative Writing (TAAS) SPP 115

- Turn to page _____ in your test booklet. Find the number _____ at the top of the page and put your finger on it. (Check to see if everyone has found the number.)
- In this lesson you will write a story that you have made up by yourself. The picture and directions will help you get started. Before you begin writing, you will use scratch paper to brainstorm and organize your ideas. Use your imagination to think up great ideas.
- Use the best English you can but do not worry about mistakes. The most important thing is to write clearly so that the person reading your story can imagine what is happening from the beginning to the end. Use the notes that you made on the scratch paper to remember your ideas and stay organized.

Teacher Scripts

Work-Study Skills: Maps (ITBS) <inline>SPP 116</inline>

- Turn to page _____ in your test booklet. Find the number _____ at the top of the page and put your finger on it. (Check to see if everyone has found the number.)

- In this lesson you will work with maps. Look at the map at the top of the page. It is the map of part of a make-believe city. Take a few minutes to look at the map. Look at what is shown and where things are located.

- Now let's talk about the map. Find the words north, south, east, and west along the edges of the map. North is always up. Which way is south? (down) Which way is west? (left) Which way is east? (right) What places do you see on the map? What streets?

- Now look at sample A. Read the question to yourself as I read it out loud. (Read the first question out loud.) Look at the map. Find Main Street running across the middle of the map. Pretend that you are walking west until just after crossing Oak Avenue. What is on your left? (the park) Fill in the answer in front of the park because that is the right answer.

- Look at sample B. Read the question to yourself. What are the key words in the question? (street, parking lot) Look at the map and find the parking lot. Which street runs alongside the parking lot? (Oak Avenue) Fill in the circle in front of Oak Avenue.

- Look at the next map and its set of questions. This is a road map. Take a few moments to study the map. Look at what is shown and where things are located. Also, study the key to the map. (pause) Now we will finish this page. Read each question to yourself as I read it aloud. Then look at the map to find the answer. Fill in the circle in front of the best answer for each question.

Work-Study Skills: Graphs/Tables (ITBS) <inline>SPP 117</inline>

- Turn to page _____ in your test booklet. Find the number _____ at the top of the page and put your finger on it. (Check to see if everyone has found the number.)

- In this lesson you will work with graphs and tables. Find the graph at the top of the page. It shows how many tasks five students completed in a science center. Study the graph for a few moments. (pause) Now look at sample A. Read the question to yourself as I read it out loud. As we read, look for key words. Remember, key words are words in the question that help you find the answer. (Read the question for sample A out loud.)

- What are the key words in this question? (how many, Mario, complete) Use the graph to find the answer to the question. Look at the row of stars for Mario and count them. How many tasks did Mario complete? (three) Now look at the answers. Fill in the circle in front of the numeral 3 because Mario completed three tasks.

- Now look at sample B. Read the question to yourself and look for key words. What are the key words in this question? (same number, as Gina) Look at the graph. How many tasks did Gina complete? (four) Who completed the same number of tasks as Gina? (Rick) Fill in the circle in front of Rick because the graph shows that Gina and Rick both completed four tasks.

- Move down to the table near the middle of the page. Carefully read each question along with me. Then look at the table to find the answer. Fill in the circle in front of the answer you choose for each question.

Teacher Scripts

Work-Study Skills: Alphabetizing (SAT/MAT) SPP 118

- Turn to page _____ in your test booklet. Find the number _____ at the top of the page and put your finger on it. (Check to see if everyone has found the number.)

- In this lesson you will think about the alphabetical order of words. Put your marker under sample A at the top of the page. Look at the three words: penny . . . dog . . . king. Which word comes first in alphabetical (or ABC) order? (dog) The correct answer is the second word, dog, because it comes before the other words in alphabetical order. Fill in the circle in front of the word dog.

- Put your marker under sample B in the second column. Look at the three words: bring . . . brought . . . brown. Which word comes first in alphabetical (or ABC) order? (bring) The correct answer is the first word, bring, because it comes before the other words in alphabetical order. Fill in the circle in front of the word bring.

- Now we are going to do the rest of this page. Listen closely to each set of words that I read. Fill in the circle beside the word that comes first in alphabetical (or ABC) order.

- Put your marker on number 1 in the first column. Choose the word that comes first in alphabetical (or ABC) order: friend . . . funny . . . fort.

- Move your marker on number 2. Choose the word that comes first in alphabetical (or ABC) order: stand . . . star . . . step.

- Move your marker on number 3. Choose the word that comes first in alphabetical (or ABC) order: hand . . . many . . . jam.

- Move your marker on number 4. Choose the word that comes first in alphabetical (or ABC) order: throw . . . three . . . thrill.

- Move your marker on number 5. Choose the word that comes first in alphabetical (or ABC) order: present . . . cake . . . birthday.

- Move your marker on number 6 near the top of the second column. Choose the word that comes first in alphabetical (or ABC) order: stop . . . go . . . wait.

- Move your marker on number 7. Choose the word that comes first in alphabetical (or ABC) order: train . . . window . . . yellow.

- Move your marker on number 8. Choose the word that comes first in alphabetical (or ABC) order: rain . . . ran . . . rattle.

- Move your marker on number 9. Choose the word that comes first in alphabetical (or ABC) order: wind . . . little . . . tree.

- Move your marker on number 10. Choose the word that comes first in alphabetical (or ABC) order: computer . . . calculator . . . printer.

Teacher Scripts

Work-Study Skills: Alphabetical Order (ITBS)   `SPP 119`

- Turn to page _____ in your test booklet. Find the number _____ at the top of the page and put your finger on it. (Check to see if everyone has found the number.)

- Pretend that you are making a dictionary page, using the pictures at the top of this paper. In your mind, imagine cutting out the pictures and gluing them onto a piece of paper in alphabetical, or ABC, order. Put the first word at the top of the dictionary page and the last word at the bottom.

- Find sample A. Read the question to yourself while I read it out loud: Which picture should be at the very top of the page? Look at the pictures to find the answer. (the apple) The picture of the apple should be at the top of the page because it comes first in alphabetical order. Fill in the second answer circle.

- Look at sample B. Read the question to yourself while I read it out loud: Which picture should be between the rabbit and the zebra? Look at the pictures to find the answer. (the watch) The picture of the watch should be between the rabbit and the zebra because w comes between r and z in the alphabet. Fill in the third answer circle.

- Now we will finish the page. Read each question to yourself as I read it out loud. Look at the pictures. Then fill in the answer circle for your choice.

- Move to number 1. Which picture should be the second one on the page?

- Move to number 2. Which picture should be right after the watch?

- Move to number 3. Which picture should be right before the hoe?

- Move to number 4 near the top of the second column. Which picture should be between the apple and the dog?

- Move to number 5. Which picture should be right after the dog?

- Move to number 6. Which picture should be the last one on the page?

Work-Study Skills: Table of Contents   `SPP 120`

- Turn to page _____ in your test booklet. Find the number _____ at the top of the page and put your finger on it. (Check to see if everyone has found the number.)

- On this page you will work with the tables of contents of books. Find the table of contents at the top of this page. It is from a book about mountains. Take a few moments to read the table of contents. Now look at sample A. Read the question to yourself as I read it out loud. As we read, look for key words that will help you find the answer. (Read the question out loud.)

- What are they key words in this question? (which pages, skiing) Which chapter do you think tells about skiing? (Chapter 1, Winter Sports) Find Chapter 1 on the left side of the table of contents. Now read across to the right side where the page numbers are listed. On which page does Chapter 1 begin? (page 1) The number under 1 is 10. That means the next chapter begins on page 10. If the next chapter begins on page 10, on which page does Chapter 1 end? (9) So Chapter 1 is on pages 1 through 9. Look at the answers. Fill in the circle in front of 1–9 because you could probably learn about skiing on these pages

- Find the table of contents in the middle of the page. It is from a book about Alaska. Take a few moments to read the table of contents.

- Now we are ready to finish this page. Read each question to yourself as I read it aloud. Then look at the table of contents to find the answer. Fill in the circle in front of the best answer for each question. (Read each question aloud to the students.)

Teacher Scripts

Work-Study Skills: Classifying (ITBS)

SPP 121

- Turn to page _____ in your test booklet. Find the number _____ at the top of the page and put your finger on it. (Check to see if everyone has found the number.)

- On this page you will think about how things are the same and how they are different. Look at sample A. There are four pictures in the sample. What are they? (a lighted candle, a lamp, a flashlight, a computer) One of the pictures does not go with the other pictures. Which picture is it? (the computer) Why? (A computer is the only one that is not used to give light.) Fill in the circle under the computer.

- Look at sample B. There are four words in this sample. One of the words does not go with the other words. Which word is it? (happy) Why? (Happy is a word for how you feel; the other words are names for things you do.) Fill in the circle under the word happy because it does not go with the other words.

- Do the rest of the page by yourself. Name the pictures or read the words in each set. Fill in the answer circle under the word or picture that does not go with the others.

Work-Study Skills: Reference Materials (ITBS)

SPP 122

- Turn to page _____ in your test booklet. Find the number _____ at the top of the page and put your finger on it. (Check to see if everyone has found the number.)

- On this page you will decide on the best places to find different kinds of information. Look at sample A. Read the question to yourself as I read it out loud. The information in the question will help you choose an answer.

- What are you being asked to find? (a way to get to a local museum) Now read the answer choices to yourself as I read them out loud: at a clock . . . on a globe . . . on a street map. If you want to get to a local museum, should you look at a clock, on a globe, or on a street map? (street map) Yes, a street map can tell you how to get to a local museum. Fill in the circle in front of on a street map because that is the best answer.

- Now look at sample B. Read the question to yourself. What are you being asked to find? (a book that will give information about elephants) Read the answers. Which answer names a book you could use to learn about elephants? (a book about wild animals) Fill in the circle in front of the second answer.

- We are going to do the rest of the page in the same way that we did the samples. Read the question and answer choices in each item to yourself as I read them out loud. Fill in the circle in front of each answer you choose. (Read the questions and answer choices aloud to the students.)

Teacher Scripts

Math: Computation—Addition (No Regrouping)

- Turn to page _____ in your test booklet. Find the number _____ at the top of the page and put your finger on it. (Check to see if everyone has found the number.)
- In this lesson you will be finding answers to addition problems. Look at the problem in sample A. You are being asked to add 5 and 3. Look at the four answer choices next to the problem. What are they? (53, 8, 9, and 2) One of these numbers is the answer to the problem. Now work out the problem and find its answer. If you want to do any figuring, do it on the scratch paper that I gave to you. What is 5 plus 3? (8) Yes, 8 is the right answer. Fill in the circle next to the number 8 because 5 plus 3 is 8. Do not write the number 8 under the problem in your book.
- Now look across the page to sample B. It shows another way to write an addition problem. What numbers are you being asked to add? (1, 6, and 2) Now work out the problem. Do your figuring on your scratch paper, not in your book. How much is 1 plus 6 plus 2? (9) Yes, 1 plus 6 plus 2 equals 9. Look at the answers. Fill in the answer circle next to 9 because 9 is the right answer. Do not write the answer after the equal sign at the end of the problem.
- Work by yourself to do the rest of the page. Add each problem carefully. Then fill in the answer circle next to the answer to the problem. Use your scratch paper to do any figuring that you need to do. Do not write the answers in your booklet.

Math: Computation—Addition (Regrouping)

- Turn to page _____ in your test booklet. Find the number _____ at the top of the page and put your finger on it. (Check to see if everyone has found the number.)
- In this lesson you will be finding answers to addition problems. Look at the problem in sample A. You are being asked to add 6 and 5. Look at the four answer choices next to the problem. What are they? (13, 11, 1, and 12) One of these numbers is the answer to the problem. Now work out the problem and find the answer. If you want to do any figuring, do it on the scratch paper that I gave to you. What is 6 plus 5? (11) Yes, 11 is the right answer. Fill in the circle next to the number 11 because 6 plus 5 equals 11. Do not write the number 11 under the problem in your book.
- Now look across the page to sample B. It shows another way to write an addition problem. What numbers are you being asked to add? (42 and 28) The problem might be easier if you do your figuring on your scratch paper. If you copy the problem onto your scratch paper, make sure that you line the numbers up correctly. Write the 8 in 28 under the 2 in 42 and the 2 in 28 under the 4 in 42. Now work out the problem. Be sure to add carefully. What is 42 plus 28? (70) Look at the answer choices. Fill in the answer circle in front of 70 because 70 is the right answer. Do not write the answer after the equal sign at the end of the problem.
- Work by yourself to do the rest of the page. Add each problem carefully. Then fill in the answer circle next to the answer to the problem. Use your scratch paper to do any figuring that you need to do. Do not write the answers in your booklet.

Teacher Scripts

Math: Computation—Subtraction (No Regrouping)   SPP 125

- Turn to page _____ in your test booklet. Find the number _____ at the top of the page and put your finger on it. (Check to see if everyone has found the number.)

- In this lesson you will be finding answers to subtraction problems. Look at the problem in sample A. The problem asks you to find the answer to 6 minus 4. Look at the four answer choices next to the problem. What are they? (10, 6, 4, and 2) One of these numbers is the answer to the problem. Now work out the problem to find the correct answer. If you want to do any figuring, do it on the scratch paper that I gave to you. What is 6 minus 4? (2) Yes, 2 is the right answer. Fill in the circle next to the number 2 because 6 minus 4 is 2. Do not write the number 2 under the problem in your booklet.

- Now look across the page to sample B. What does the problem ask you to do? (subtract 6 from 77) This problem will be easier to do if you copy it onto scratch paper first. Copy the numbers carefully. Be sure to line up the numbers correctly. Now work out the problem. Look at the answer choices and find the answer. What is 77 minus 6? (71) Yes, 71 is the right answer so you should fill in the answer circle next to 71.

- Work by yourself to do the rest of the page. Subtract carefully on each problem. Then fill in the circle next to the answer to the problem. Use your scratch paper to do any figuring. Do not write the answers in your booklet.

Math: Computation—Subtraction (Regrouping)   SPP 126

- Turn to page _____ in your test booklet. Find the number _____ at the top of the page and put your finger on it. (Check to see if everyone has found the number.)

- In this lesson you will be finding answers to subtraction problems. Look at the problem in sample A. What are you being asked to do? (subtract 56 from 82) Look at the four answer choices. What are they? (136, 36, 26, and 32) One of these numbers is the correct answer to the problem. Copy it carefully onto your scratch paper. Be sure to write the 2 in 52 under the 4 in 84 and the 5 in 52 under the 8 in 84. Now work out the problem. (pause) What is 84 minus 52? (32) Fill in the circle next to the number 32 because 84 minus 52 is 32. Do not write the number 32 under the problem in your booklet.

- Now look across the page to sample B. What does the problem ask you to do? (subtract 8 from 63) This problem will be easier to do if you copy it onto scratch paper first. Copy the numbers carefully and be sure to line up the 8 under the 3 in 63. Work out the problem now. (pause) Look for your answer among the answer choices. What is 63 minus 8? (55) Fill in the circle next to the number 55 because 63 minus 8 is 55.

- Work by yourself to do the rest of the page. Subtract carefully on each problem. Then fill in the circle next to the answer to the problem. Use your scratch paper to do any figuring. Do not write the answers in your booklet.

Teacher Scripts

Math: Computation—Multiplication (with Pictures)   SPP 127

- Turn to page _____ in your test booklet. Find the number _____ at the top of the page and put your finger on it. (Check to see if everyone has found the number.)

- This lesson is about multiplication. Look at the directions at the top of the page. Read them to yourself as I read them aloud.

- Let's do the sample. Mr. Wilson gave 2 candy bars each to Franklin, Pham, and Jose. How many candy bars did he give them in all? Which answer choice tells how many candy bars Mr. Wilson gave the boys? (6) Yes, the third answer, 6, is correct because there were 3 boys and each boy received 2 candy bars. Fill in the circle beside the second answer.

- Now we will finish the page. Read the problems to yourself as I read them out loud. Remember to read each question carefully, look at the picture that is part of the question, and then look at each answer choice. Fill in the circle next to your answer choice.

Math: Computation—Multiplication   SPP 128

- Turn to page _____ in your test booklet. Find the number _____ at the top of the page and put your finger on it. (Check to see if everyone has found the number.)

- In this lesson you will find the answers to multiplication problems. Look at sample A. What are you being asked to do? (multiply 4 and 7) Look at the answer choices. What are they? (11, 74, 28, 21, none of these) You should fill in the circle in front of *none of these* only if the right answer is not given as one of the answer choices. Now multiply the problem carefully. Use scratch paper if you need to. What is 4 times 7? (28) Look at the answers. Is 28 one of the answer choices? (yes) Fill in the circle in front of 28 because 4 times 7 is 28.

- Look at sample B. What are you being asked to do? (multiply 31 and 2) Now work out the problem. Copy it carefully onto your scratch paper first. Line up the numbers so that the 2 is under the 1 in 31. Then multiply carefully. What is 31 times 2? (62) Yes, 62 is the right answer. Look at the answer choices. Is 62 one of the choices? (no) The right answer is not given in your book, so you should fill in the circle in front of *none of these*.

- Finish this page by yourself. Do the rest of the problems in the same way that we did the samples. If you need to, use scratch paper to work out the problems. Fill in the circle next to the answer that you choose for each problem. Do not write the answers in your booklet.

Teacher Scripts

Math: Computation—Division (with Pictures) | SPP 129 |

- Turn to page _____ in your test booklet. Find the number _____ at the top of the page and put your finger on it. (Check to see if everyone has found the number.)

- This lesson is about division. Look at the directions at the top of the page. Read them to yourself as I read them aloud.

- Let's do the sample. There are 6 ice cream bars in a package. A group of 3 friends wanted to share the package so that they each would get the same number of ice cream bars. How many ice cream bars would each friend get? Which answer shows how many ice cream bars each friend would get? (the first answer) Yes, the first answer, 2, is correct because each friend would get 2 ice cream bars. Fill in the circle beside the first answer.

- Now we will finish the page. Read the problems to yourself as I read them out loud. Remember to read each question carefully, look at the pictures that are part of the question, and then look at each answer choice. Fill in the circle next to your answer choice.

Math: Computation—Division | SPP 130 |

- Turn to page _____ in your test booklet. Find the number _____ at the top of the page and put your finger on it. (Check to see if everyone has found the number.)

- In this lesson you will find the answers to division problems. Look at sample A. What are you being asked to do? (divide 84 by 4) Another way to think about this problem is to ask yourself, "How many 4s are there in 84? Look at the answer choices. What are they? (12, 20, 23, 31, none of these) Remember, you should fill in the circle in front of *none of these* only if the right answer is not given as one of the answer choices in your book. Now work out the problem. Copy it exactly onto your scratch paper and divide carefully. What is 84 divided by 4? (21) Yes, 84 divided by 4 is 21. Look at the answer choices. Do you see 21? (no) Then what should you do? Fill in the circle in front of *none of these*.

- Look at sample B. This is another way of writing a division problem. What are you being asked to do in sample B? (divide 9 by 6) Look at the answer choices. Two of them have remainders. The capital letter *R* stands for the word remainder. Be careful when you work out the problem. Your answer may have a remainder. It will be easier to do if you rewrite $9 \div 6$ as $6\overline{)9}$. Then divide carefully. What answer did you get? (1 remainder 3) To check that your answer is correct, multiply 1 and 6 and then add the remainder 3. Did you get 9? (yes) Look at the answer choices. Remember, the letter *R* stands for remainder. Is 1 *R* 3 given as an answer choice? (yes) Fill in the circle in front of 1 R 3 because 9 divided by 6 is 1 remainder 3.

- Finish the page by yourself. Do the rest of the problems in the same way that we did the samples. If you need to, use scratch paper to work out the problems. Fill in the circle next to the answer you choose for each problem. Do not write the answers in your book.

Teacher Scripts

Math: Concepts/Applications—Patterns/Sequence/Order SPP 131

- Turn to page _____ in your test booklet. Find the number _____ at the top of the page and put your finger on it. (Check to see if everyone has found the number.)
- In this lesson you will work with patterns. Look at the sequence of objects in sample A. Which object should come next to make a pattern? (a circle) Fill in the circle under the object that should come next.
- Move down to number 1. Look at the sequence of the objects. Which object should come next to make a pattern? Fill in the circle under the object that should come next.
- Move down to number 2. Look at the sequence of the objects. Which object should come next to make a pattern? Fill in the circle under the object that should come next.
- Move down to number 3. Look at the sequence of objects. Which object should come next to make a pattern? Fill in the circle under the object that should come next.

Math: Concepts/Applications—Numeration SPP 132

- Turn to page _____ in your test booklet. Find the number _____ at the top of the page and put your finger on it. (Check to see if everyone has found the number.)
- In this lesson you will work with numbers. Look at the picture in the sample. I am going to read a problem about the picture. As I read, listen for key words. Key words are the important words in a problem. They will help you find the answers. Listen carefully and look at sample A. Find the number that shows how many circles are in the box. What are the key words in the problem? (how many, in the box) Now look at the answer choices next to the picture. Which number tells how many circles are in the box? (25) Fill in the circle under the number 25 to show that there are 25 circles in the box.
- Now we are going to finish the page. You are going to do more problems in the same way that we did the sample. I will read each problem to you. If you need to, use your scratch paper to figure out the answers. When you have finished working on a problem, fill in the circle for your answer choice.
- Find number 1. Look at the numbers above the circles. Which number goes in the blank? Fill in the circle for your answer.
- Move down to number 2. Find the number 59. Fill in the circle under your answer.
- Move down to number 3. Here are four different ways to write numbers. Find the smallest number. Fill in the circle for your answer.
- Move down to number 4. Look at the number sentence. Find the number that goes in the box to make the number sentence true. Fill in the circle for your answer.
- Move down to number 5. Look at the four numbers. Find the number that has a 4 in the hundreds place. Fill in the circle for your answer.
- Move down to number 6. Look at the four horses standing in a line. Fill in the circle under the horse that is third in line.

Teacher Scripts

Math: Concepts/Applications—Number Families

- Turn to page _____ in your test booklet. Find the number _____ at the top of the page and put your finger on it. (Check to see if everyone has found the number.)

- In this lesson you will work with families of facts. Look at the equations (or number sentences) in the sample. They are part of a family of facts. Which equation (or number sentence) is needed to make the fact family complete? ($9 - 5 = 4$) Yes, families of facts in addition and subtraction have two addition equations (or number sentences) and two subtraction equations (or number sentences). The same three numbers appear in all of the equations (or number sentences). Mark the circle below the second answer choice, $9 - 5 = 4$.

- Find number 1. Study the equations. Three of them belong to the same family of facts. Which one does not belong? Fill in the circle under the one that does not belong.

- Move down to number 2. Which one of these facts is in the same number family as $4 + 3 = 7$? Fill in the answer circle under the fact that is in the same number family as $4 + 3 = 7$.

- Move down to number 3. Look at the number sentence in the box. Find the missing fact among the answer choices. Fill in the answer circle under the number fact that is missing from the box.

- Move down to number 4. Study the equations. Three of them belong to the same family of facts. Which one does not belong? Fill in the circle under the one that does not belong.

- Move down to number 5. Which one of these facts is in the same number family as $8 + 7 = 15$? Fill in the answer circle under the fact that is in the same number family as $8 + 7 = 15$.

- Move down to number 6. Look at the number facts in the box. Find the missing fact among the answer choices. Fill in the circle under the number fact that is missing from the box.

Math: Concepts/Applications—Number Sentences/Theory (1)

- Turn to page _____ in your test booklet. Find the number _____ at the top of the page and put your finger on it. (Check to see if everyone has found the number.)

- In this lesson you will work with number sentences. Look at sample A. Read the problem. In this problem you need to find the number that belongs in the box to make the number sentence true. Look at the number sentence under the question. What number plus 7 equals 11? (4) Now look at the answer choices. Fill in the circle in front of the number 4 because 4 will make the number sentence true.

- Look at sample B. Read the question and look at the number sentence. In this question, 2 plus what number equals 6? (4) Now look at the answer choices. Fill in the circle in front of the number 4 because 4 will make the number sentence true.

- Work by yourself to finish the rest of the page. In each item choose the number that will make the number sentence true. Fill in the circle in front of your answer choice.

Teacher Scripts

Math: Concepts/Applications—Number Sentences/Theory (2) SPP 135

- Turn to page _____ in your test booklet. Find the number _____ at the top of the page and put your finger on it. (Check to see if everyone has found the number.)
- In this lesson you will work with numbers and number sentences. Look at sample A. Read the problem and the number sentence. In this problem you will need to find the sign that goes in the box to make the number sentence true. Look at the first answer choice, the plus sign. Let's try putting the plus sign in place of the box. Use your scratch paper to see if 8 plus 10 equals 9 plus 2. What is 8 plus 10? (18) What is 9 plus 2? (11) Does 18 equal 11? (No) Now try the next answer choice, the minus sign. Does 8 plus 10 equal 9 minus 2? (no) The next choice is the *multiplication sign*. What is 9 times 2? (18) Does 8 plus 10 equal 9 times 2? (yes) The multiplication sign makes the sentence true. Fill in the circle in front of the *multiplication sign*.
- Look at sample B. In this problem listen for key words. What are key words? (the important words in a problem) Read the problem. What are the key words in this problem? (two even numbers) Check each answer choice carefully and find the one with two even numbers. Which answer choice shows two even numbers? (the last one) What are the numbers? (4 and 14) Fill in the circle in front of the last answer choice.
- Work by yourself to finish the rest of the page. For each item fill in the circle in front of your answer choice.

Math: Concepts/Applications—Whole Numbers SPP 136

- Turn to page _____ in your test booklet. Find the number _____ at the top of the page and put your finger on it. (Check to see if everyone has found the number.)
- In this lesson you will work with numbers. Look at the four answer choices in sample A. I am going to read the directions for this item. As I read, listen for the key words and numbers. Do not mark your answer yet. Just listen and look at the numbers. Find the numeral that is 10 greater than 53. What are the key words and numbers in the directions? (10 greater than 53) Which answer shows the numeral that is 10 greater than 53? (the third answer, 63) Fill in the circle under the third answer because 63 is 10 greater than 53.
- Look at sample B. Listen for the key words and numbers as I read the directions. Find the numeral that is nearest in value to 423. What are the key words and numbers? (nearest in value, 423) Finding the numeral that is nearest in value to 423 is the same as finding the numeral that is closest to 423. The numeral may be larger or smaller than 423. Look at the answers. Fill in the answer circle under the numeral that is closest in value to 423. Which answer did you mark? (425) Yes, of the answers given, 425 is closest in value to 423.
- Now you are going to do more problems in the same way that we did the sample items. Listen carefully to the directions for each item. Then fill in the circle for your answer.
- Item 1: Look at the picture. Which number sentence describes the picture? Fill in the circle for your answer.
- Item 2: Which number sentence shows that 9 is greater than 6? Fill in the circle for your answer.
- Item 3: Fill in the answer circle under 56.
- Item 4: Look at the subtraction sentence. Fill in the circle under the best estimate of the answer.
- Item 5: Look at the number lines. Which number line shows 9 minus 3 equals 6? Fill in the circle for your answer.
- Find item 6 near the top of the next column. Look at the numeral in the box. Fill in the circle in front of the word name for the numeral.
- Item 7: Fill in the answer circle for the numeral that is 5 less than 29.
- Item 8: Fill in the answer circle under the sum of 7 and 5.
- Item 9: Fill in the answer circle for the numeral that comes between 23 and 28.
- Item 10: The words in the box say three thousand fourteen. Which numeral shows this number? Fill in the circle for your answer.

Teacher Scripts

Math: Concepts/Applications—Place Value

SPP 137

- Turn to page _____ in your test booklet. Find the number _____ at the top of the page and put your finger on it. (Check to see if everyone has found the number.)
- In this lesson you will answer questions about place value. Look at the large numeral in sample A. Now look at the four answer choices. What are they? (ones, tens, hundreds, thousands) What is the place value of 8 in the numeral? (hundreds, 8 is in the hundreds place) Fill in the circle under the word hundreds.
- Look at sample B. Which numeral has 4 tens and 9 ones? (the second one, 49) Fill in the answer circle under 49 because it has 4 tens and 9 ones.
- Find item 1. Look at the large numeral. What is the place value of 7 in this numeral? Fill in the circle under your answer choice.
- Move down to item 2. Which numeral has 2 hundreds, 1 ten, and 8 ones? Fill in the circle under your answer choice.
- Move down to item 3. Look at the large numeral. What is the place value of 5 in this numeral? Fill in the circle under your answer choice.
- Move down to item 4. Which numeral has 5 hundreds, 6 tens, and 3 ones? Fill in the circle under your answer choice.
- Move down to item 5. Which numeral has 7 hundreds, 2 tens, and 3 ones? Fill in the circle under your answer choice.
- Move down to item 6. How many tens are in 1,562 . . . 1,562? Fill in the circle under your answer choice.
- Move down to item 7. How many tens are in 3,849 . . . 3,849? Fill in the circle under your answer choice.
- Move down to item 8. How many tens are in 1,025 . . . 1,025? Fill in the circle under your answer choice.

Math: Concepts/Applications—Fractions

SPP 138

- Turn to page _____ in your test booklet. Find the number _____ at the top of the page and put your finger on it. (Check to see if everyone has found the number.)
- In this lesson you will work with fractions. Look at the four shapes in sample A. Part of each shape is filled in. I am going to read the directions for sample A. Listen carefully. Find the shape that has one-third filled in. When you work with fractions, the parts of a shape must be equal. How many equal parts does the word *thirds* mean? (three) How many of the three parts should be filled in to show one-third? (one) Now look at the answers. Which shape has one-third filled in? (the third one) Fill in the answer circle under the third shape because it has one-third filled in.
- Now look at the four sets of squares in sample B. Which set has three-fourths of the squares filled in? (the second one) The second set is correct because there are 4 squares and 3 of them or three-fourths are filled in. Fill in the circle under the second set of squares because it shows three-fourths of the squares filled in.
- Find item 1. Mark the answer circle under the shape that is filled in to show one-fourth.
- Move down to item 2. Mark the answer circle under the set that has one-eighth of the squares filled in.
- Move down to item 3. Mark the answer circle under the shape that is filled in to show one-half.
- Move down to item 4. Mark the answer circle under the set that has one-half of the squares filled in.
- Move down to item 5. Mark the answer circle under the shape that is filled in to show two-thirds.
- Find item 6 near the top of the second column. Mark the answer circle under the set that has two-thirds of the squares filled in.
- Move down to item 7. Mark the answer circle under the shape that is filled in to show one-sixth.
- Move down to item 8. Mark the answer circle under the set that has one-tenth of the squares filled in.
- Move down to item 9. Mark the answer circle under the shape that is filled in to show three-fourths.
- Move down to item 10. Mark the answer circle under the set that has one-fourth of the squares filled in.

Teacher Scripts

Math: Concepts/Applications—Money (1)

SPP 139

- Turn to page _____ in your test booklet. Find the number _____ at the top of the page and put your finger on it. (Check to see if everyone has found the number.)

- In this lesson you will work with money. Look at the group of coins in the sample. Who can name the coins? (one quarter, one dime, one nickel, three pennies) What is the value of this group of coins? (43 cents) Look at the answers. Which answer circle should you fill in? (the third one) The third answer is correct because the value of this group of coins is 43 cents.

- Work by yourself to do the rest of this page. In each item figure out the value of the coins and then fill in the circle below the correct answer.

Math: Concepts/Applications—Money (2)

SPP 140

- Turn to page _____ in your test booklet. Find the number _____ at the top of the page and put your finger on it. (Check to see if everyone has found the number.)

- In this lesson you will work with money. Look at the sample. Who can name the coins in this sample? (dime, nickel, penny, quarter) Now listen to the directions. Find the coin that is worth more than 2 cents but less than 10 cents. Look at the coins again. What is the value of a dime? (10 cents) A penny? (1 cent) A nickel? (5 cents) A quarter? (25 cents) Which coin is worth more than 2 cents but less than 10 cents? (the nickel) Fill in the answer circle under the third coin, the nickel.

- Find item 1. Look at the coins. Which coin is worth more than 15 cents but less than 30 cents? Fill in the circle under the coin that you choose.

- Find item 2. Look at the coins. Which coin is worth more than 5 cents but less than 20 cents? Fill in the circle under the coin that you choose.

- Find item 3. Look at the coins. Which coin is worth less than 5 cents? Fill in the circle under the coin that you choose.

- Find item 4. Look at the coins. Which set of coins is worth more than 15 cents but less than 25 cents? Fill in the circle under the set of coins that you choose.

- Find item 5. Look at the coins. Which set of coins is worth more than 70 cents but less than 80 cents? Fill in the circle under the set of coins that you choose.

Teacher Scripts

Math: Concepts/Applications—Graphs

- Turn to page _____ in your test booklet. Find the number _____ at the top of the page and put your finger on it. (Check to see if everyone has found the number.)

- In this lesson you will work with graphs. Look at the graph at the top of the page. Listen carefully. Marcia lives in Hawaii where it rains a little almost every day. Marcia decided to keep track of the days when there was no rain at all. She kept a record for six months during the spring and summer. Each picture of a sun means a day that had no rain at all. Use the graph to do items A, B, and C.

- Find item A at the top of the right column. Read the question to yourself as I read it out loud. In which month were there the fewest dry days? (September) Use the graph to find out. Fill in the circle in front of your answer.

- Move down to item B. Read the question to yourself as I read it out loud. How many more dry days were there in May than in August? (2) Use the graph to find out. Fill in the circle in front of your answer.

- Move down to item C. Read the question to yourself as I read it out loud. How many dry days were there in May and June altogether? (9) Use the graph to find out. Fill in the circle in front of your answer.

- Look at the second graph. Some of the students in Mrs. Black's class kept track of the books they read by making a graph. Each picture of a book stands for two books read. Use this graph to do items 1, 2, 3, and 4.

- Find item 1 in the middle of the page. Read the question to yourself as I read it out loud. How many books did Lili read? Use the graph to find out. Fill in the circle in front of your answer.

- Move down to item 2. Read the question to yourself as I read it out loud. Which two students read the same number of books? Use the graph to find out. Fill in the circle in front of your answer.

- Move down to item 3. Read the question to yourself as I read it out loud. How many more books did Sung read than Kris? Use the graph to find out. Fill in the circle in front of your answer.

- Move down to item 4. Read the question to yourself as I read it out loud. How many books did the students read in all? Use the graph to find out. Fill in the circle in front of your answer.

Teacher Scripts

Math: Concepts/Applications—Geometry (1) | SPP 142 |

- Turn to page _____ in your test booklet. Find the number _____ at the top of the page and put your finger on it. (Check to see if everyone has found the number.)
- In this lesson you will work with shapes. Find sample A. Look at the shapes while I read the directions. Fill in the answer space under the square. Which answer did you choose? (the last one) Yes, a square has four sides that are the same length.
- Look across the page at sample B. Look at the envelope. Then look at the shapes. Fill in the answer space under the shape that is most like the shape of the envelope. Which space did you mark? (the rectangle) The shape of the envelope is most like a rectangle.
- Now find item 1. Fill in the answer space under the triangle.
- Move down to item 2. Fill in the answer space under the circle.
- Move down to item 3. Fill in the answer space under the shape that looks most like a teepee.
- Move down to item 4. Fill in the answer space under the shape that looks most like a flag.
- Move down to item 5. Look at the first shape. Then look at the shapes next to it. Fill in the answer space under the shape that looks the same as the inside of the first shape but is larger.
- Find item 6 near the top of the second column. Fill in the answer space under the shape that has no corners.
- Move down to item 7. Look at the first picture. A shape is being cut out of a folded piece of paper. Fill in the answer space under the shape that will be cut out.
- Move down to item 8. Fill in the answer space under the picture that shows a circle in a square.
- Move down to item 9. Fill in the answer space under the number that tells how many sides a triangle has.
- Move down to item 10. Fill in the answer space under the picture that shows a triangle in a circle.

Math: Concepts/Applications—Geometry (2) | SPP 143 |

- Turn to page _____ in your test booklet. Find the number _____ at the top of the page and put your finger on it. (Check to see if everyone has found the number.)
- In this lesson you will work with shapes. Look at the shapes in sample A. Which one has the same shape as the first one in the row? (the third one) Fill in the answer space under the third shape because it is the same as the first one in the row.
- Look at the shapes in sample B. If you folded each shape along its dotted line, which shape would have sides that matched exactly? (the circle) Fill in the circle under the shape that would have matching sides.
- Move down to item 1. Look at the shape. Fill in the answer space under the word that names the shape.
- Move down to item 2. Look at the shapes. If you folded each shape along its dotted line, only one shape would have sides that matched exactly. Fill in the answer space under the shape that would have matching sides.
- Move down to item 3. Look at the shapes. Fill in the answer space under the figure with the same size and shape as the first one in the row.
- Move down to item 4. Look at the shape. Fill in the answer space under the word that names the shape.
- Move down to item 5. Look at the shape. Fill in the answer space under the word that names the shape.
- Move down to item 6. Fill in the answer space under the open box that would hold the most groceries.
- Move down to item 7. Look at the shapes. If you folded each shape along its dotted line, only one shape would have sides that matched exactly. Fill in the answer space under the shape that would have matching sides.

Teacher Scripts

Math: Concepts/Applications: Measurement (1)

SPP 144

- Turn to page _____ in your test booklet. Find the number _____ at the top of the page and put your finger on it. (Check to see if everyone has found the number.)

- In this lesson you will work with measurement. Find the sample. Look at the pictures and name them. (scale, thermometer, clock, ruler) Andy wants to know how warm it is outside. Which picture shows what Andy should use to find the temperature? (the thermometer) Fill in the circle under the picture of the thermometer because Andy could use it to find the temperature outside.

- Move down to item 1. Peaches are on sale at the grocery store. Mrs. Brown wants to buy four big peaches. Which picture shows what Mrs. Brown should use to find out how much the peaches weigh? Fill in the circle under what Mrs. Brown should use.

- Move down to item 2. School starts at nine o'clock. What should James use to find out how much time he has to get ready? Fill in the circle under what James should use.

- Move down to item 3. Find the picture of someone or something that is about six feet tall. Fill in the answer circle.

- Move down to item 4. Jan needs 18 inches of ribbon for a project she is doing. Which picture shows what Jan should use to measure the ribbon? Fill in the circle under the picture of what Jan should use.

- Move down to item 5. How many inches are in a foot? Fill in the circle below the number that tells how many inches are in a foot.

- Move down to item 6. How many feet are in a yard? Fill in the circle below the number that tells how many feet are in a yard.

Math: Concepts/Applications—Measurement (2)

SPP 145

- Turn to page _____ in your test booklet. Find the number _____ at the top of the page and put your finger on it. (Check to see if everyone has found the number.)

- In this lesson you will work with clocks. Find sample A. Look at the clock. Remember, the little hand tells the hour and the big hand tells the minutes. What time is shown on the clock? (3:40) Fill in the circle next to 3:40.

- Look at sample B. Find the digital clock that shows the same time as the round clock. Look at the round clock. What time does it show? (12:30) Which digital clock should you choose? (the first one) Fill in the circle next to the first digital clock.

- Move down to number 1. What time does the clock show? Fill in the circle next to your answer.

- Move down to number 2. Find the round clock that shows the same time as the digital clock. Fill in the circle under your answer.

- Move down to number 3. What time does the clock show? Fill in the circle next to your answer.

- Move down to number 4. What time does the clock show? Fill in the circle next to your answer.

- Move down to number 5. What time does the clock show? Fill in the circle next to your answer.

- Move down to number 6. Find the round clock that shows the same time as the digital clock. Fill in the circle under your answer.

Teacher Scripts

Math: Concepts/Applications—Measurement (3) **SPP 146**

- Turn to page _______ in your test booklet. Find the number _______ at the top of the page and put your finger on it. (Check to see if everyone has found the number.)
- In this lesson you will work with a calendar. Take a moment to look at the month from a calendar at the top of the page. Use this calendar month to answer the questions.
- Find item 1. This month begins on which day of the week? Fill in the circle under your answer.
- Move down to item 2. On which day of the week does March 17 fall? Fill in the circle under your answer.
- Move down to item 3. The fourth Friday of this month falls on which date? Fill in the circle under your answer.
- Move down to item 4. How many days does March have? Fill in the circle under your answer.

Math: Concepts/Applications—Measurement (4) **SPP 147**

- Turn to page _______ in your test booklet. Find the number _______ at the top of the page and put your finger on it. (Check to see if everyone has found the number.)
- In this lesson you will measure length, temperature, and weight. Look at item 1. Study the Celsius thermometer. What temperature is shown on this thermometer? Fill in the circle next to your answer.
- Move down to item 2. Study the scale. How much does the rock weigh? Fill in the circle next to your answer.
- Move down to item 3. Study the pencil and the ruler. How long is this pencil? Fill in the circle next to your answer.
- Move down to item 4. Study the stick and the ruler. How long is the stick? Fill in the circle next to your answer.

Math: Concepts/Applications—Problem Solving (Adding with Pictures) **SPP 148**

- Turn to page _______ in your test booklet. Find the number _______ at the top of the page and put your finger on it. (Check to see if everyone has found the number.)
- On this page you will do some word problems. Let's do the sample together. Kim had two buttons on her dress. Her mother sewed on two more buttons. Find the answer that shows how many buttons in all were on Kim's dress. (pause) Which answer did you choose? (the first one) Right. Fill in the circle under the answer that shows four buttons.
- Move down to item 1. Three cars were parked in a parking lot. Three more cars parked in the same parking lot. Find the number sentence that shows how you could find out how many cars in all were parked in the parking lot. Fill in the circle under your answer choice.
- Move down to item 2. Mrs. West had a package of ten small plants for her flower garden. She bought two more plants. How many plants did she have in all? Fill in the circle under your answer choice.
- Move down to item 3. Six ants crawled out of an anthill. Four more ants crawled out to join them. How many ants crawled out of the anthill in all? Fill in the circle under your answer choice.
- Move down to item 4. There were two eggs in a nest. The mother bird laid three more eggs. How many eggs were in the nest altogether? Fill in the circle under your answer choice.
- Move down to item 5. There were two fish in one bowl and three fish in another bowl. How many fish were there in all? Fill in the circle under your answer choice.
- Move down to item 6. One butterfly was on a branch. Two more butterflies flew nearby. How many butterflies were there in all? Fill in the circle under your answer choice.

Teacher Scripts

Math: Concepts/Applications—Problem Solving
(Subtracting with Pictures)

SPP 149

- Turn to page _____ in your test booklet. Find the number _____ at the top of the page and put your finger on it. (Check to see if everyone has found the number.)
- On this page you will do some word problems. Let's do the sample together. Look at the birds. There were five birds on the ground. Two of the birds flew away. How many birds were left on the ground? (pause) Which answer did you choose? (the second one, three) Right. Fill in the circle under the second answer.
- Move down to item 1. Mario had five pears. He gave three pears to Joe. How many pears did Mario have left? Fill in the circle under your answer choice.
- Move down to item 2. Mark gave his dog, Sparky, six dog biscuits. Sparky ate two of them right away. How many biscuits did Sparky have left? Fill in the circle under your answer choice.
- Move down to item 3. Jason had seven cookies in his lunch. If he gave four cookies to his friend, how many cookies would Jason have left for himself? Fill in the circle under your answer choice.
- Move down to item 4. Six children were playing in the yard. Two of them went home for lunch. How many children were still playing in the yard? Fill in the circle under your answer choice.
- Move down to item 5. Howard had three books. He gave one of them to Frank. How many books did Howard have left? Fill in the circle under your answer choice.
- Move down to item 6. Lisa had 10 blocks. She stacked up seven of them. How many blocks did Lisa not use in her stack? Fill in the circle under your answer choice.

Math: Concepts/Applications—Problem Solving
(Addition)

SPP 150

- Turn to page _____ in your test booklet. Find the number _____ at the top of the page and put your finger on it. (Check to see if everyone has found the number.)
- On this page you will do some word problems. Let's do the sample together. Look at the problem while I read it out loud. Mrs. Taylor planted 6 pink rose bushes and 5 white rose bushes in her front yard. Which number sentence tells how to find the number of rose bushes she planted altogether? How would you find the answer to this problem? (add 6 and 5) What is the sum of 6 and 5? (11) Now look for the number sentence that says the same thing. Which answer would you choose? $(6 + 5 = 11)$ Fill in the circle under the fourth answer.
- Now I will read each problem out loud. Listen carefully.
- Item 1: Maria bought 5 candy bars on Monday. On Wednesday she bought 3 more. How many candy bars did Maria buy in all? Fill in the circle next to your answer choice.
- Item 2: Ron has 5 baseball cards, 7 football cards, and 2 soccer cards. How many sports cards does Ron have in all? Fill in the circle next to your answer choice.
- Item 3: Lin and José were playing checkers. Lin won 6 games and José won 4 games. How many games did they play? Fill in the circle next to your answer choice.
- Item 4: At the Springton Zoo Reptile House there are 11 lizards, 25 snakes, and 7 turtles. How many reptiles are there in all? Fill in the circle next to your answer choice.
- Item 5: Gus bought 2 tickets to the high school play. The tickets cost $4 each. Which number sentence tells how to find out how much money Gus spent altogether? Fill in the circle next to your answer choice.
- Item 6: In the morning there were seven crows on the old oak tree. In the afternoon eight more crows joined them. How many crows were in the old oak tree in all? Fill in the circle next to your answer choice.

Teacher Scripts

Math: Concepts/Applications—Problem Solving (Subtraction)

SPP 151

- Turn to page _____ in your test booklet. Find the number _____ at the top of the page and put your finger on it. (Check to see if everyone has found the number.)
- On this page you will do some word problems. Let's do the sample together. Look at the problem while I read it out loud. On the east side of Oak Tree Lane there are 12 houses. There are 9 houses on the west side. How many more houses are there on the east side? How would you find the answer to this problem? (Subtract 9 from 12.) What is the answer? (3) Fill in the circle next to 3.
- Now I will read each problem out loud. Listen carefully.
- Item 1: On Sunday, 35 children were playing in the park. Then 14 of them went home. How many children were still playing? Fill in the circle next to your answer choice.
- Item 2: Jesse bought a bat for $13. He paid for it with a $20 bill. How much change did he get back? Fill in the circle next to your answer choice.
- Item 3: Fred colored 24 Easter eggs. He colored 12 of them yellow and 12 of them blue. Fred gave 18 of them away to his friends. Which number sentence tells how to find the number of Easter eggs he had left? Fill in the circle next to your answer choice.
- Item 4: Martha set the dinner table for 9 people. Only 7 people were able to come for dinner. How many sets of silverware should Martha take off of the table? Fill in the circle next to your answer choice.
- Item 5: A group of 12 people planned to pick up their tickets at the box office on the night of the big game. Only 8 of these people made it to the game and 5 of them were late. How many tickets were left at the box office? Fill in the circle next to your answer choice.
- Item 6: There were 55 students who tried out for the school play. Only 33 students got parts. Which number sentence tells how to find out how many students did not get parts? Fill in the circle next to your answer choice.

Math: Concepts/Applications—Problem Solving (Multiplication)

SPP 152

- Turn to page _____ in your test booklet. Find the number _____ at the top of the page and put your finger on it. (Check to see if everyone has found the number.)
- On this page you will do some word problems. Let's do the sample together. Look at the problem while I read it out loud. The city planted two trees in front of each house on Main Street. There are 28 houses on Main Street between 2nd and 3rd Avenues. How many trees were planted on that part of Main Street? How would you find the answer to this problem? (Multiply 28 by 2.) What is the answer? (56) Fill in the circle next to 56.
- Now I will read each problem out loud. Listen carefully.
- Item 1: Zach has been invited to 3 birthday parties. He wants to give 5 baseball cards to each person who is having a birthday. Which number sentence can be used to find out how many cards Zach should buy? Fill in the circle next to your answer choice.
- Item 2: A train has 12 passenger cars, 2 dining cars, and 3 baggage cars. Each passenger car has 9 people in it. How many people are traveling on the train altogether? Fill in the circle next to your answer choice.
- Item 3: Room 24 had a class party. There are 28 children in the class. How many cookies did they need in order to give 3 cookies to each student? Fill in the circle next to your answer choice.
- Item 4: Mrs. Ray was setting up a science experiment. She placed two slides by each of the 16 microscopes on the desks. Which number sentence shows how to find the number of slides she placed on the desks? Fill in the circle next to your answer choice.
- Item 5: There are 14 teams in Benny's baseball league. There are 10 children on each team. Every team will play 20 games during the season. How many children belong to the league? Fill in the circle next to your answer choice.
- Item 6: The students were getting ready for a banquet. They expected 48 people to attend. They placed 3 decorations on each of the 8 tables. How many decorations did they use in all? Fill in the circle next to your answer choice.

Teacher Scripts

Math: Concepts/Applications—Two-Step Problem Solving SPP 153

- Turn to page _____ in your test booklet. Find the number _____ at the top of the page and put your finger on it. (Check to see if everyone has found the number.)

- On this page you will do some word problems. Let's do the sample together. Look at the problem while I read it out loud. The ages of the three children in the Ramirez family add up to 17. Charles, the oldest boy, is 10. Lupe, the middle child, is 6. How old is the baby? How would you find the answer to this problem? (add 10 and 6, subtract that answer from 17) Yes, this is a two-step problem. What is the answer? (1) Fill in the circle next to 1.

- Now I will read each problem out loud. Listen carefully.

- Item 1: Jeff has $4 to buy 2 bottles of ketchup for the class picnic. The ketchup costs $1.20 a bottle. How much money will Jeff have left after he buys the ketchup? Fill in the circle next to your answer choice.

- Item 2: Della has 22 sports cards. She has 7 baseball cards and 8 football cards. The rest of the cards are soccer cards. How many soccer cards does Della have? Fill in the circle next to your answer choice.

- Item 3: Chan made 17 origami frogs. He gave 5 to Lin and 3 to Maria. How many frogs did Chan have left? Fill in the circle next to your answer choice.

- Item 4: Gary's allowance is $5 a week and Shamika's is $4 a week. Over a period of 4 weeks, how much more money does Gary receive? Fill in the circle next to your answer choice.

- Item 5: Marilyn and her family went on a vacation for 14 days. They spent 5 days in Germany and 4 days in Italy. They spent the rest of the time in France. How many days did they spend in France? Fill in the circle next to your answer choice.

- Item 6: Javier saved $50 to buy new clothes for school. He bought a shirt for $14 and a pair of jeans for $12. How much money does Javier have left for shoes? Fill in the circle next to your answer choice.

Math: Concepts/Applications—Estimation SPP 154

- Turn to page _____ in your test booklet. Find the number _____ at the top of the page and put your finger on it. (Check to see if everyone has found the number.)

- On this page you will do some estimation problems. Let's do the sample together. Look at the problem while I read it out loud. Look at the price list below. About how much does a bunch of green onions cost? Notice that the question asks you to find about how much a bunch of onions costs. You do not have to find the exact answer. Which answer should you choose? ($.30) Fill in the circle next to $.30.

- Now I will read each problem out loud. Listen carefully.

- Item 1: One place mat costs $1.95. About how much would 6 place mats cost? Fill in the circle next to your answer choice.

- Item 2: A box measures 18 inches on each side. About how much ribbon would you need to go around the box once? Fill in the circle next to your answer choice.

- Item 3: Read the shopping list. Which is the best way to figure out about how much all of the items on the list would cost? Fill in the circle next to your answer choice.

Teacher Scripts

Math: Concepts/Applications—Strategies

SPP 155

- Turn to page _____ in your test booklet. Find the number _____ at the top of the page and put your finger on it. (Check to see if everyone has found the number.)

- On this page you will figure out some strategies or ways of doing problems. Let's do the sample together. Look at the problem while I read it out loud. Suppose you had 2 jars full of buttons. Which answer shows the way to find the number of buttons altogether in both jars? Notice that you are being asked how to do the problem. Which answer should you choose? (the first one, you would add the buttons in each jar together)

- Now I will read each problem out loud. Listen carefully.

- Item 1: How would you find the distance around this figure? Fill in the circle next to your answer choice.

- Item 2: A pitcher holds 16 ounces of lemonade. You poured two 4-ounce glasses of lemonade for yourself and a friend. How could you find out how much is left in the pitcher? Fill in the circle next to your answer choice.

- Item 3: Read the shopping list. Which is the best way to figure out exactly how much all of the items on the list would cost? Fill in the circle next to your answer choice.

Math: Concepts/Applications—Reasonable Answers

SPP 156

- Turn to page _____ in your test booklet. Find the number _____ at the top of the page and put your finger on it. (Check to see if everyone has found the number.)

- On this page you will figure out some answers that make sense. Let's do the sample together. Look at the problem while I read it out loud. About how high is a regular door? Look at the answer choices. There are 12 inches in one foot which is about this high. (demonstrate) There are 36 inches in 3 feet or one yard. Seven feet is a foot taller than many adult men and 15 feet is taller than two men together. Which answer makes the most sense? (7 feet) Fill in the circle next to 7 feet.

- Now I will read each problem out loud. Listen carefully.

- Item 1: About how long is an average-size car? Fill in the circle next to your answer choice.

- Item 2: Pretend you are using a calculator to multiply 10 x 100. How many zeroes will be in the answer? Fill in the circle next to your answer choice.

- Item 3: Imagine that you are setting the dinner table for 6 people. Each person will get 3 pieces of silverware: a knife, a fork, and a spoon. Which answer shows how many pieces of silverware you will need altogether? Fill in the circle next to your answer choice.

Answer Key

Page 31
1. ○ ○ ● ○
2. ○ ○ ○ ●
3. ○ ○ ● ○
4. ○ ● ○ ○
5. ● ○ ○ ○
6. ○ ○ ○ ●
7. ○ ● ○ ○

Page 32
1. ○ ○ ● ○
2. ● ○ ○ ○
3. ○ ○ ○ ●
4. ○ ○ ○ ●
5. ● ○ ○ ○
6. ○ ○ ● ○
7. ○ ○ ○ ●

Page 33
1. ○ ● ○
2. ○ ● ○
3. ○ ● ○
4. ○ ● ○
5. ● ○ ○
6. ○ ● ○
7. ● ○ ○

Page 34
1. ○ ○ ○ ●
2. ○ ○ ○ ●
3. ○ ○ ○ ●
4. ○ ○ ● ○
5. ○ ● ○ ○
6. ○ ○ ● ○
7. ○ ● ○ ○
8. ● ○ ○ ○

Page 35
1. ○ ●
2. ● ○
3. ○ ●

Page 36
1. ○ ○ ●
2. ○ ○ ●

3. ○ ○ ●
4. ○ ○ ●
5. ○ ● ○
6. ● ○ ○

Page 37
1. ○ ● ○
2. ○ ○ ●
3. ○ ○ ●
4. ● ○ ○
5. ○ ● ○
6. ○ ● ○

Page 38
1. ○ ○ ●
2. ○ ○ ●
3. ● ○ ○
4. ● ○ ○
5. ○ ● ○
6. ● ○ ○

Page 39
1. ● ○ ○ ○
2. ○ ● ○ ○
3. ○ ● ○ ○
4. ○ ○ ○ ●
5. ○ ● ○ ○
6. ○ ● ○ ○
7. ● ○ ○

Page 40
1. ○ ○ ○ ●
2. ● ○ ○ ○
3. ○ ○ ○ ●
4. ● ○ ○ ○
5. ○ ○ ● ○
6. ○ ● ○ ○
7. ○ ● ○

Page 41
1. ○ ● ○
2. ○ ○ ●
3. ○ ○ ●
4. ○ ○ ●
5. ○ ● ○
6. ● ○ ○

Page 42
1. ○ ○ ● ○
2. ○ ● ○ ○
3. ○ ● ○ ○
4. ○ ○ ● ○
5. ○ ○ ● ○
6. ● ○ ○ ○
7. ○ ○ ○ ●
8. ○ ● ○ ○
9. ● ○ ○ ○
10. ○ ○ ○ ●
11. ● ○ ○ ○
12. ○ ● ○ ○
13. ○ ● ○ ○
14. ● ○ ○ ○

Page 43
1. ○ ○ ●
2. ● ○ ○
3. ○ ● ○
4. ○ ○ ●
5. ● ○ ○
6. ○ ● ○

Page 44
1. ● ○ ○
2. ○ ● ○
3. ○ ● ○
4. ○ ● ○
5. ● ○ ○
6. ○ ○ ●
7. ○ ● ○

Page 45
1. ● ○ ○ ○
2. ○ ○ ● ○
3. ○ ○ ○ ●
4. ● ○ ○ ○
5. ○ ● ○ ○
6. ○ ○ ● ○
7. ○ ○ ● ○

Page 46
1. ● ○ ○ ○
2. ○ ● ○ ○

Page 47
1. ○ ○ ● ○
2. ○ ● ● ○
3. ○ ● ○ ○
4. ○ ○ ○ ●
5. ○ ● ○ ○
6. ○ ○ ● ○
7. ● ○ ○ ○

Page 48
1. ● ○ ○ ○
2. ● ○ ○ ○
3. ● ○ ○ ○
4. ○ ● ○ ○
5. ● ○ ○ ○
6. ○ ● ○ ○
7. ● ○ ○ ○

Page 49
1. ○ ○ ● ○
2. ○ ○ ○ ●
3. ○ ○ ○ ●
4. ○ ○ ○ ●
5. ○ ○ ○ ●
6. ○ ○ ● ○
7. ○ ○ ○ ●

Page 50

1. ○	2. ○	3. ○
○	●	●
●	○	○
4. ○	5. ○	6. ●
●	●	○
○	○	○
7. ●	8. ●	
○	○	
○	○	

Answer Key *(cont.)*

Page 51
1. ○ ○ ○ ●
2. ○ ● ○ ○
3. ○ ○ ○ ●
4. ● ○ ○ ○
5. ○ ● ○ ○
6. ○ ○ ● ○
7. ○ ○ ● ○

Page 52
1. ● ○ ○
2. ○ ● ○
3. ○ ○ ●
4. ● ○ ○
5. ○ ● ○
6. ○ ○ ●
7. ● ○ ○
8. ○ ○ ●

Page 53
1. ● ○ ○ ○
2. ○ ○ ● ○
3. ● ○ ○ ○
4. ○ ● ○ ○
5. ● ○ ○ ○
6. ○ ● ○ ○
7. ● ○ ○ ○

Page 54
1. ○ ● ○
2. ○ ○ ●
3. ○ ● ○
4. ○ ○ ●

Page 55
1. ● ○ ○
2. ● ○ ○
3. ○ ● ○
4. ○ ● ○
5. ● ○ ○
6. ○ ○ ●

Page 56
1. ○ ● ○ ○
2. ● ○ ○ ○
3. ○ ● ○ ○
4. ○ ○ ○ ●
5. ○ ● ○ ○
6. ○ ○ ● ○
7. ● ○ ○ ○

Page 57
1. ○ ○ ○ ●
2. ○ ● ○ ○
3. ● ○ ○ ○
4. ○ ○ ● ○
5. ● ○ ○ ○
6. ○ ○ ○ ●
7. ● ○ ○ ○

Page 58
1. ●   2. ○   3. ○
   ○   ○   ○
   ○   ●   ●
4. ●   5. ○   6. ●
   ○   ●   ○
7. ●   8. ○
         ●

Page 59
1. ●   2. ○   3. ○
   ○   ○   ●
   ○   ●   ○
4. ●   5. ○   6. ○
   ○   ○   ●
   ○   ●   ○
7. ●   8. ○
         ●
         ○

Page 60
1. ○   2. ●   3. ○
   ●   ○   ●
   ○   ○   ○
4. ●   5. ○   6. ○
   ○   ●   ○
   ○   ○   ●
7. ○   8. ○
   ○   ●
   ●   ○

Page 61
1. ●   2. ○   3. ●
   ○   ○   ○
   ○   ●   ○
4. ○   5. ○   6. ○
   ○   ○   ●
   ○   ●   ○
   ●   ○   ○

Page 62
1. ○ ● ○ ○
2. ● ○ ○ ○
3. ○ ○ ● ○
4. ○ ● ○ ○
5. ○ ● ○ ○

Page 63
1. ● ○ ○ ○
2. ○ ● ○ ○
3. ○ ● ○ ○
4. ○ ○ ○ ●
5. ● ○ ○ ○

Page 64
1. ○   2. ○   3. ○
   ○   ●   ●
   ○   ○   ○
   ●   ○   ○
4. ●   5. ○   6. ○
   ○   ●   ○
   ○   ○   ●
   ○   ○   ○

Page 65
1. ○ ● ○
2. ○ ● ○
3. ○ ○ ●
4. ● ○ ○
5. ○ ○ ●

Page 66
1. ○ ○ ●
2. ○ ○ ●
3. ● ○ ○
4. ○ ● ○
5. ● ○ ○

Page 67
1. ●   2. ○   3. ○
        ●   ○
        ○   ●
4. ○
   ●
   ○

Page 68
1. ● ○ ○
2. ○ ○ ●
3. ○ ● ○
4. ○ ● ○
5. ● ○ ○
6. ○ ○ ●
7. ○ ● ○
8. ○ ● ○
9. ○ ○ ●
10. ○ ● ○
11. ○ ● ○
12. ● ○ ○
13. ○ ● ○
14. ○ ● ○

Page 69
1. ● ○ ○
2. ● ○ ○
3. ● ○ ○
4. ○ ● ○
5. ● ○ ○
6. ○ ● ○

Page 70
1. ● ○ ○
2. ○ ○ ●
3. ● ○ ○
4. ○ ● ○
5. ○ ● ○

Answer Key *(cont.)*

Page 71
1. ○   2. ○   3. ○
   ●   ○   ●
   ○   ●   ○
4. ●
   ○
   ○

Page 72
1. ○ ○ ● ○
2. ● ○ ○ ○
3. ○ ○ ○ ●
4. ○ ● ○ ○
5. ○ ○ ● ○

Page 73
1. ○   2. ●   3. ●
   ○   ○   ○
   ○   ○
   ●   ○
4. ○
   ○
   ●
   ○

Page 74
1. ○ ○ ● ○
2. ○ ● ○ ○
3. ● ○ ○ ○
4. ○ ○ ○ ●

Page 75
5. ●   6. ○   7. ○
   ○   ○   ●
   ○   ●   ○
8. ○
   ○
   ○
   ●

Page 76
9. ○   10. ○   11. ●
   ●   ○   ○
   ○   ○
   ○   ●

12. ○
   ●
   ○
   ○

Page 77
1. ○   2. ○   3. ○
   ●   ○   ○
   ○   ○   ○
   ○   ●   ●
4. ●

Page 78
5. ●   6. ●   7. ○
   ○   ○   ●
   ○   ○
   ○   ○
8. ●
   ○
   ○
   ○

Page 79
9. ○   10. ○   11. ○
   ○   ●   ●
   ○   ○
   ●   ○
12. ○
   ○
   ○
   ●

Page 80
1. ○   2. ○   3. ●
   ○   ●   ○
   ●   ○   ○
4. ○
   ○
   ○
   ●

Page 81
5. ●   6. ○   7. ●
   ○   ○   ○
   ○   ○   ○
   ○   ●   ○
8. ○
   ●

Page 82
9. ○   10. ●   11. ●
   ○   ○   ○
   ○   ○
   ●   ●
12. ○
   ●
   ○
   ○

Page 83
1. ○   2. ○   3. ●
   ●   ○   ○
   ○   ●   ○
   ○   ○   ○
4. ○
   ●
   ○
   ○

Page 84
5. ●   6. ●   7. ○
   ○   ○   ○
   ○   ○   ●
   ○   ○
8. ○
   ●
   ○
   ○

Page 85
9. ●   10. ○   11. ○
   ○   ○   ●
   ○   ○
   ○   ●

12. ○
   ●
   ○
   ○

Page 86
1. ○ ○ ●
2. ○ ● ○
3. ○ ● ○
4. ● ○ ○
5. ○ ● ○

Page 87
1. ●   2. ○   3. ○
   ○   ●   ○
   ○   ○   ●
4. ●   5. ○   6. ○
   ○   ●   ○
   ○   ○   ●
7. ○   8. ○
   ●   ●
   ○   ○

Page 88
1. ○ ● ○
2. ○ ○ ●
3. ● ○ ○
4. ● ○ ○
5. ○ ○ ●
6. ○ ○ ●
7. ● ○ ○
8. ● ○ ○
9. ○ ● ○
10. ○ ○ ●

Page 89
1. ○   2. ○   3. ○
   ○   ●   ●
   ●   ○   ○
4. ●   5. ○   6. ○
   ○   ○   ○
   ○   ●   ●

Answer Key (cont.)

7.○ 8.○ 9.●
  ● ○ ○
  ○ ● ○
10.○
  ●
  ○

Page 90
1.○ 2.○ 3.○
  ○ ○ ●
  ○ ○ ○
  ● ● ○
4.○ 5.○ 6.○
  ○ ○ ●
  ● ○ ○
  ○ ● ○
7.○ 8.○ 9.●
  ○ ○ ○
  ● ● ○
10.○
  ○
  ○
  ●

Page 91
1.○ 2.○ 3.○
  ○ ● ●
  ● ○ ○
  ○ ○ ○
4.● 5.○ 6.●
  ○ ○ ○
  ○ ● ○
  ○ ○ ○
7.○ 8.○ 9.○
  ○ ○ ●
  ● ● ○
  ○ ○ ○
10.○
  ○
  ●
  ○

Page 92
1. ○ ○ ●
2. ● ○ ○
3. ○ ○ ●
4. ● ○ ○
5. ○ ○ ●
6. ○ ○ ●
7. ○ ○ ●
8. ○ ● ○

Page 93
1. ○ ○ ● ○
2. ● ○ ○ ○
3. ○ ○ ● ○
4. ○ ● ○ ○

Page 94
1. ● 2. ○ 3. ●
  ○ ● ○
  ○ ○ ○
4. ○ 5. ○ 6. ●
  ○ ○ ○
  ● ● ○

Page 95
1. ○ 2. ● 3. ○
  ○ ○ ●
  ● ○ ○
4. ○ 5. ○ 6. ○
  ● ○ ○
  ○ ● ○
7. ● 8. ○
  ○ ○
  ○ ●

Page 96
1. Sunday I
2. Louis
3. Cay
4. The
5. —
6. Arch
7. —
8. Mississippi
9. —

10. —
11. Dear Marcie
12. Girl
13. —
14. I
15 Mrs. Watson
16. —
17. Can
18. Friday, May
19. —
20. Your

Page 97
1. ○ ○ ● ○ ○
2. ○ ○ ○ ● ○
3. ● ○ ○ ○ ○
4. ○ ○ ● ○ ○
5. ● ○ ○ ○ ○
6. ○ ○ ○ ○ ●
7. ○ ○ ○ ● ○

Page 98
1. ○ 2. ○ 3. ●
  ● ○ ○
  ○ ● ○
4. ○ 5. ● 6. ○
  ● ○ ○
  ○ ○ ●
7. ● 8. ●
  ○ ○
  ○ ○

Page 99
1. none
2. of?
3. it?
4. none
5. see?
6. zoo.
7. none
8. "Let's
9. shopping."
10. none
11. Reno,

12. May 5,
13. skating,
14. none
15. Bill's, doesn't
16. none
17. none
18. Hooray!"

Page 100
1. ○ 2. ○ 3. ○
  ○ ○ ●
  ○ ○ ○
  ● ● ○
4. ● 5. ○ 6. ○
  ○ ○ ○
  ○ ● ○
  ○ ○ ○
7. ○ 8. ○
  ○ ○
  ● ●
  ○ ○

Page 101
1. ○ 2. ○ 3. ○
  ○ ○ ●
  ○ ● ○
  ● ○ ○
4. ○ 5. ○ 6. ○
  ○ ○ ○
  ○ ● ○
  ● ○ ●

Page 102
1. ○ 2. ○ 3. ○
  ● ○ ○
  ○ ● ○
  ○ ○ ●
4. ●
  ○
  ○
  ○
  ○

Page 103
1. ○ 2. ○ 3. ●
  ● ● ○

Answer Key *(cont.)*

Page 103 (cont.)

4. ○ ○	5. ○ ●		
● ○	○ ○		
6. ○ ○	7. ○ ○		
● ○	● ○		
8. ○ ○	9. ○ ●		
● ○	○ ○		
10. ● ○	11. ●		
○ ○	○		
12. ●	13. ○ ●		
○	○ ○		
14. ●	15. ●		
○	○		
16. ● ○			
○ ○			

Page 104

1. ○	2. ○	3. ○
○	○	○
●	●	●
○	○	○
4. ●	5. ●	6. ○
○	●	○
○	○	●
○	○	○

Page 105

1. ○	2. ○	3. ●
●	●	○
○	○	○
○	○	○
4. ●	5. ●	6. ○
○	○	●
○	○	○
7. ○	8. ○	
○	○	
●	●	
○	○	

Page 106

1. ○	2. ○	3. ●
●	○	○
○	●	○

4. ○	5. ●	6. ●
●	○	○
○	○	○
7. ○	8. ○	9. ●
●	●	○
○	○	○
10. ○		
●		
○		

Page 107

1. ○	2. ○	3. ●
○	○	○
●	●	○
4. ●	5. ●	6. ●
○	○	○
○	○	○
7. ●	8. ○	9. ○
○	●	●
10. ○		
●		
○		

Page 108

1. ● ○ ○
2. ○ ● ○
3. ○ ○ ●
4. ○ ● ○
5. ○ ○ ●
6. ● ○ ○

Page 109

1. ●	2. ●	3. ○
○	○	○
○	○	●
4. ●	5. ○	6. ○
○	●	●
○	○	○
7. ○	8. ○	9. ●
○	●	○
●	○	○
10. ○		
●		
○		

Page 110

1. ○ ○ ● ○
2. ○ ● ○ ○
3. ○ ○ ● ○
4. ○ ● ○ ○

Page 111

1. ○	2. ●	3. ●
●	○	○
4. ●	5. ○	6. ○
○	●	●

Page 112

1. ○	2. ○	3. ●
●	○	○
○	●	○
4. ●	5. ○	6. ○
○	○	●
○	●	○

Page 116

1. ● ○ ○
2. ○ ● ○
3. ● ○ ○

Page 117

1. ○ ○ ●
2. ○ ● ○
3. ○ ● ○
4. ● ○ ○
5. ○ ● ○

Page 118

1. ○	2. ●	3. ●
○	○	○
●	○	○
4. ●	5. ○	6. ○
○	○	●
○	●	○
7. ●	8. ●	9. ○
○	○	●
○	○	○

Page 119 (cont.)

10. ○
    ●
    ○

Page 119

1. ● ○ ○
2. ○ ● ○
3. ○ ○ ●
4. ○ ● ○
5. ○ ● ○
6. ● ○ ○

Page 120

1. ○	2. ●	3. ○
●	○	●
○	○	○
4. ○		
○		
●		

Page 121

1. ● ○ ○ ○
2. ○ ● ○ ○
3. ○ ○ ○ ●
4. ○ ○ ● ○
5. ○ ● ○ ○
6. ○ ○ ● ○
7. ○ ○ ○ ●

Page 122

1. ○	2. ○	3. ○
○	○	●
○	●	○
4. ○	5. ●	6. ○
●	○	●
○	○	○

Page 123

1. ○	2. ○	3. ○
○	○	●
●	○	○
4. ●	5. ○	6. ●
○	●	○

Answer Key *(cont.)*

7.● 8.○ 9.○
  ○   ○   ●
  ○   ●   ○
  ○   ○   ○
10.○
  ○
  ●
  ○

Page 124
1.○ 2.○ 3.○
  ○   ○   ●
  ●   ●   ○
  ○   ○   ○
4.● 5.○ 6.○
  ○   ○   ○
  ○   ●   ○
  ○   ○   ●
7.○ 8.○ 9.○
  ○   ○   ○
  ●   ●   ○
  ○   ○   ●
10.○
  ●
  ○
  ○

Page 125
1.● 2.○ 3.○
  ○   ○   ○
  ○   ●   ●
  ○   ○   ○
4.○ 5.○ 6.○
  ○   ●   ●
  ○   ○   ○
  ○   ○   ○
7.○ 8.○ 9.○
  ○   ○   ○
  ●   ●   ○
  ○   ○   ●
10.○
  ●
  ○
  ○

Page 126
1.○ 2.○ 3.●
  ○   ○   ○
  ○   ○   ○
  ●   ●   ○
4.○ 5.○ 6.●
  ●   ○   ○
  ○   ●   ○
  ○   ○   ○
7.● 8.○ 9.○
  ○   ○   ○
  ○   ●   ●
  ○   ○   ○
10.●
  ○
  ○
  ○

Page 127
1.○○ 2.○○
  ●○   ○●
3.○○
  ○●

Page 128
1.● 2.● 3.○
  ○   ○   ●
  ○   ○   ○
  ○   ○   ○
4.○ 5.○ 6.○
  ○   ○   ○
  ●   ○   ●
  ○   ●   ○
7.○ 8.● 9.○
  ○   ○   ○
  ○   ○   ●
  ●   ○   ○
10.○
  ○
  ●
  ○

Page 129
1.○● 2.○○
  ○○   ●○
3.○○
  ●○

Page 130
1.○ 2.○ 3.○
  ○   ●   ●
  ●   ○   ○
  ○   ○   ○
4.○ 5.○ 6.○
  ●   ○   ○
  ○   ○   ●
  ○   ●   ○
7.● 8.● 9.○
  ○   ○   ○
  ○   ○   ●
  ○   ○   ○
10.○
  ●
  ○
  ○

Page 131
1.○○●
2.○○●
3.●○○

Page 132
1.○●○○
2.○○●○
3.●○○○
4.○○●○
5.○●○○
6.○○●○

Page 133
1.○○○●
2.●○○○
3.○○○●

4.○○●○
5.○○●○
6.○○○●

Page 134
1.●○ 2.○○
      ●○
3.○○ 4.○○
  ●○   ○●
5.●○ 6.●○

Page 135
1.○● 2.○●
      ○○
3.○○
  ●○
4.○
  ●
  ○
  ○
5.●○ 6.○○
  ○○   ●○

Page 136
1.●○
  ○○
2.○
  ○
  ○
  ●
3.○○○●
4.○●○○
5.○
  ●
  ○
  ○
6.○
  ○
  ○
  ●
7.○○●○
8.○●○○
9.○○●○
10.●○○○

Answer Key *(cont.)*

Page 137
1. ○ ● ○ ○
2. ○ ○ ○ ●
3. ● ○ ○ ○
4. ○ ● ○ ○
5. ● ○ ○ ○
6. ○ ○ ● ○
7. ○ ○ ○ ●
8. ○ ○ ● ○

Page 138
1. ● ○ ○ ○
2. ○ ● ○ ○
3. ● ○ ○ ○
4. ○ ○ ● ○
5. ○ ● ○ ○
6. ○ ○ ○ ●
7. ○ ○ ○ ●
8. ● ○ ○ ○
9. ○ ○ ○ ●
10. ○ ○ ● ○

Page 139
1. ○ ○ ● ○
2. ○ ● ○ ○
3. ○ ○ ○ ●
4. ○ ○ ○ ●
5. ○ ○ ○ ●

Page 140
1. ○ ● ○ ○
2. ○ ○ ○ ●
3. ● ○ ○ ○
4. ○ ○ ● ○
5. ○ ● ○ ○

Page 141
1. ○ ○   2. ● ○
   ○ ●   ○ ○
3. ○ ○   4. ○ ○
   ○ ●   ○ ●

Page 142
1. ○ ● ○ ○
2. ● ○ ○ ○
3. ○ ● ○ ○
4. ○ ○ ● ○
5. ● ○ ○ ○
6. ● ○ ○ ○
7. ○ ● ○ ○
8. ○ ● ○ ○
9. ○ ● ○ ○
10. ○ ● ○ ○

Page 143
1. ○ ○ ● ○
2. ○ ○ ● ○
3. ○ ○ ○ ●
4. ○ ○ ● ○
5. ○ ○ ○ ●
6. ○ ○ ● ○
7. ● ○ ○ ○

Page 144
1. ● ○ ○ ○
2. ○ ○ ● ○
3. ○ ● ○ ○
4. ○ ○ ○ ●
5. ○ ● ○ ○
6. ○ ○ ● ○

Page 145
1. ○ ○
   ●
2. ● ○ ○ ○
3. ○ ○   4. ○ ○
   ● ○   ● ○
5. ○ ●
   ○ ○
6. ○ ● ○ ○

Page 146
1. ○ ● ○ ○
2. ○ ● ○ ○
3. ○ ○ ● ○
4. ○ ○ ○ ●

Page 147
1. ● ○   2. ○ ●
   ○ ○   ○ ○
3. ○
   ○
   ●
   ○
4. ○
   ○
   ●
   ○

Page 148
1. ○ ● ○ ○
2. ○ ○ ● ○
3. ○ ○ ○ ●
4. ○ ○ ○ ●
5. ● ○ ○ ○
6. ○ ○ ● ○

Page 149
1. ● ○ ○ ○
2. ○ ○ ● ○
3. ○ ● ○ ○
4. ○ ○ ● ○
5. ○ ○ ● ○
6. ○ ● ○ ○

Page 150
1. ○ ○   2. ○ ○
   ○ ●   ○ ●
3. ● ○   4. ○ ●
   ○ ○   ○ ○
5. ○ ●   6. ○ ○
   ○ ○   ● ○

Page 151
1. ● ○   2. ○ ○
   ○ ○   ○ ●
3. ○ ●   4. ● ○
   ○ ○   ○ ○
5. ○ ○   6. ○ ●
   ○ ●   ○ ○

Page 152
1. ○ ○   2. ○ ○
   ● ○   ● ○
3. ○ ○   4. ○ ●
   ● ○   ○ ○
5. ○ ●   6. ○ ●
   ○ ○   ○ ○

Page 153
1. ○ ○   2. ● ○
   ● ○   ○ ○
3. ○ ○   4. ○ ○
   ○ ●   ● ○
5. ○ ●   6. ● ○
   ○ ○   ○ ○

Page 154
1. ○   2. ○   3. ○
   ○   ○   ●
   ●   ○   ○
   ○   ●   ○

Page 155
1. ○   2. ○   3. ○
   ○   ○   ○
   ○   ●   ○
   ●   ○   ●

Page 156
1. ○   2. ○   3. ○
   ○   ○   ●
   ●   ●   ○
   ○   ○   ○